MICROMANAGEMENT

How to Solve the Problems of Growing Companies

William A. Delaney

amacom

A DIVISION OF AMERICAN MANAGEMENT ASSOCIATIONS

Library of Congress Cataloging in Publication Data

Delaney, William A
  Micromanagement; how to solve the problems of
growing companies.

  Includes index.
  I. Small business—Management.   I. Title.
HD62.7.D44   658'.022   80-69691
ISBN 0-8144-5642-1

First Printing

I wish to dedicate this book to Helen, the woman I have loved for over 23 years. Fortunately for me, she has been my wife for that period of time.

Acknowledgments

I wish to acknowledge the assistance and support of Maureen Walsh and Connie Russo, who spent many lonely hours on the difficult task of turning my terrible handwriting into a neat manuscript. Their kindness, patience, and good cheer, plus their excellent skills and quiet efficiency, have made working with them a daily pleasure.

I also wish to acknowledge the help and advice given by Peter Plender, Eric Ellingson, Lewis Corey, and especially Walter Paige, all of whom have listened patiently to me over the years and given me the benefit of their experience. A man is fortunate if he has one person with whom he can openly and freely discuss topics of mutual interest and concern, and receive wise counsel in return. I am blessed by knowing several such people.

William A. Delaney

Contents

Introduction

Just about everyone, at one time or another in his career, thinks about starting up a new business venture and doing it his own way. It makes for pleasant fantasizing, because very few people actually do it. Statistics indicate a high mortality rate during the first year or two for those who try, and these statistics are enough to frighten away many who could well succeed. Yet, in spite of the odds, some do try. Some fail and never try again; some keep trying and keep failing; and some eventually succeed, after a long and exhausting effort that many would say wasn't worth the price.

This book is intended primarily for those who either are seriously thinking about starting out on their own business venture or are already out there playing the game. I use the word "game" because running a small business is, in many respects, similar to a game. It's a game in which the winner takes all. There is no second prize. There is no reward for effort, for how hard you try. You do your thing and either you succeed or you fail. It's that simple. This book may also be of value to people who work in a small business or who deal with small business entrepreneurs, either in joint business operations or by subcontracts from larger business operations.

The entrepreneur is the key to success or failure in the small business enterprise. He is truly a different breed from all other types of managers. He is the prime motivating factor around which the whole business revolves. So it is very important for you to determine before you start whether you are an entrepreneur. Chapter 1 of this book discusses the characteristics of the entrepreneur.

The rest of this book contains items of specific interest and value to the small business person. The information presented was gathered from 15 years of experience in the operation of a small business. The examples given and mistakes made are all real. They happened either to me or to someone whom I know well and whose opinions and honesty I value and trust. In some cases, minor details have been changed to prevent identification of specific people.

There are many books on macro-economics that discuss macro-success stories. This book is oriented toward micro-economics and micromanagement. It focuses on the small, specific, individual, and everyday level. Macro-information is necessary and good, but how does a person involved in a small business read, understand, and use all of this information to his own business advantage on an individual or micro-level basis?

I remember going to the bank for a short-term loan to cover our payroll, because our accounts receivable were overdue. The bank manager told me that the interest rate had gone up 2 percent since our last short-term note, one month before. Since our company had a long and reputable association with the bank, I asked why. The bank manager said it was because of Charles de Gaulle. I replied, "What in hell has de Gaulle to do with running my business? I don't even know him!" The explanation was long and convoluted. It had something to do with France and the gold exchange rate, which caused the prime lending rate to the banks to go up, which caused the banks to raise the interest rates, and so on.

Macro-economics had affected a small business, and it was up to us on the micro-level to adjust. We called in our accounts receivable and retained more profit in the business. Now we don't borrow as often. It is this sort of micromanagement that the small business person has to do to survive and grow. One can't expect an infant to be concerned with major problems that perplex adults. The small business venture is an infant in the corporate world, and an orphan as well. It has no wise and affluent parents to protect and shield it from youthful follies. The infant corporation can't survive big mistakes as the corporate adult can. A $50,000 error can kill the baby. Managers in a large, established company can make a multi-million-dollar blunder and joke about it in the boardroom over cigars and drinks.

There is no magic secret or sure key to success. You are what you are, I am what I am, and someone else is what he is. You can't imitate another person's style; it generally does not work the same way twice. But general principles, concepts, and guidelines can be valuable. Read about what has happened to others and what they did about it. Don't read just one book on small business ventures. Read as many as you can, and then formulate your own special plan, in your own special way. Assess your own situation as it unfolds before you and use your own good judgment in deciding whether or not to apply the information you've read about. The best thing any person has going for him is good judgment and common sense, and no book can give it to you if you don't already have it. "Read not to believe or disbelieve, but to weigh and consider."

Cyrano de Bergerac said, "I may not stand tall, but I can stand alone, unaided"; that is not a bad thing to be able to say about anyone. There is one very good test to find out if it is true of you. Start a small venture. If you are still standing three to five years later, then you can, indeed, stand alone and unaided, and you will be "one up" on Cyrano. You did what he did, and you have a much more attractive nose than he had.

Note: In the text, when I use words such as "manpower" or "man month," I am referring to people, both men and women. When the words "he" or "his" are used in context such as, "Everyone has to do his part," or "Each manager is responsible for his own group and he must submit the reports on time," once again, I refer to men and women. I first attempted to use phrases such as "he/she" or "himself/herself" in the text, but it became cumbersome and, in some cases, even unreadable.

Many of our employees are women; in fact, the most senior manager in our company, a very important member of our staff, is a highly qualified woman. I certainly don't mean to exclude women from my discussion of the small business venture, and I hope all my readers, men and women, will bear with the use of the masculine pronoun to refer to people of both sexes.

1

The Entrepreneur
and the Bureaucrat

Everything has to have a beginning. Every huge enterprise or corporation was once the idea or dream of one man or woman who initiated the venture and saw it through the early stages. Many of us, at some time during our careers, consider going out on our own, so we can call the shots, be our own boss, and do things our way. Stockbrokers dream of owning their own brokerage firm; engineers dream of running their own plant or facility; accountants and lawyers dream of starting their own law firms or consulting companies.

In most cases, such dreams remain dreams—most people fail to act on them. Some of the reasons one hears for not trying are, "I have a wife and family to support, and I can't take the risk," or "I don't have enough money to get started," or "I have been here too long, I don't want to give up my seniority," or "I'm too old." Perhaps it's just as well that those ventures aren't undertaken, because the odds are against the success of any new business, especially if its leader is easily discouraged.

The prime determinants for success or failure in a new business venture (or anything in life, I believe) are the attitudes and behavior of the person who chooses to start up and lead the new enterprise. People who are hesitant to take risks for reasons such as those given above are likely to become business casualties. Even a cursory study of those who have made new ventures succeed reveals they are not the smartest or the most talented or the luckiest or the most deserving. They all have a common behavior characteristic, though, and it is *persistence*. They never give up. They don't stop striving until they reach their goals—and then they set new goals. If they fail, they come back and try again. You only have to succeed once; the number of times you fail doesn't matter, unless you give up hope, pack it all in, and stop trying. Churchill said it better in referring to Harold, who was King of England when William conquered it in 1066. Harold was killed by an arrow during the battle, and Churchill remarked that he was undefeated except by death, which does not count in honor.

Entrepreneur is a word used to describe the business leader. The dictionary defines entrepreneur as one who "organizes, operates, and assumes the risk for business ventures." The word is derived from the French word *entreprendre*, which means to undertake. No venture, business or otherwise, will survive and grow without an entrepreneur. He is the single most important person in the enterprise. In fact, he is a *sine qua non,* because without the entrepreneur, business failure is almost a certainty. Even with one in charge, success does not automatically follow—but if you want to lead a new business venture, you had better be an entrepreneur. Successful new ventures have been started by men, women, young, old, and people in midcareer, so it's never too late to try.

How do you know if you are an entrepreneur? If you can examine yourself fairly and objectively, you can determine it for yourself. However, since most of us are too kind in examining ourselves and our faults, some outside and objective assistance may be needed. There is much more to succeeding in business than a bright idea, novel approach, or new invention, as you will see as we proceed. You have to think and plan many steps ahead, as in a chess match.

The Small Business Administration (SBA) is a government agency established to give assistance and support to would-be entrepreneurs. The SBA has branch offices in every state and I'm sure that, wherever you live, you can find an SBA office within a few hours' drive. Your congressman or senator can refer you to the local agency nearest your residence and can even set up appointments for you. Don't be afraid to meet with the SBA representatives in your area. They can and will help you. It's their job, and they want you to succeed, because every new prospering enterprise helps you, your employees, and the local, state, and federal economy. The more money you make and people you hire, the more tax money the government gets in return. So you see, it is a closed loop in which everyone benefits. The SBA will advise you and will even help you get initial financing, if required, but *you* have to make the decisions and *you* succeed or fail.

Among the many documents and pamphlets the SBA will give you is one titled, *Starting and Managing a Small Business of Your Own*. Currently the third edition is in print, and it is only 95 pages, so you can read it in no time at all. I suggest you read this document very carefully before you proceed any further. The book first helps you determine whether you are the type—that is, whether you are on entrepreneur by nature. It lists the five most important characteristics that have some correlation with later success in a business venture: drive, thinking ability, human relations ability, communication ability, and technical ability.

Drive is characterized by responsibility, initiative, health, and persistence.

Thinking ability consists of original, creative, critical, and analytical thinking, and the ability to consistently think alone and unaided. Are you a self-starter or do you need others around you to cheer you on and help you over the rough spots? Do you get so depressed that you need help from others to shake it off? Do you think up new ideas, or do you expand upon others' ideas?

Human relations ability consists in being sociable, considerate of others, cheerful, tactful, and persuasive. Are you able to lead others to do a job? Can you counsel and advise people who have a variety of personal and professional problems, and help them perform successfully? Can you sell your ideas and concepts to others?

Communication ability is composed of verbal comprehension and oral and written communication. Can you speak to others to get your ideas and desires across clearly, succinctly, and promptly? Can you write well? Are your instructions, ideas, and goals clearly understood and easily followed?

Finally, we get to *technical knowledge*. You must be knowledgeable about the product, idea, or process you plan to create and sell to others. Note that the SBA puts technical knowledge last on its list of the important characteristics of the successful entrepreneur. Let's explore why that makes sense.

The old saying, "If a man invents a better mousetrap, the world will beat a path to his door," is not necessarily true. No one will buy it unless they know about it (*advertising*). You have to sell it (*marketing*), and at a profit (*pricing*). You have to be able to produce it (*manufacturing*). You have to hire and train people to build it (*human relations*). You have to pay wages, costs, and taxes (*financing*), provide a good rate of return to yourself and to your investors (*accounting*), and obey the many state, local, and federal regulations (*legal*). So there's much more to success than just a good idea or a new product. The person whose strengths are limited to technical expertise won't last too long as the entrepreneur of a new business. One of the other areas, if left unattended, will eventually catch up with the "technical-only entrepreneur." He'll run short of money, encounter a tax problem, violate some unknown regulation, or confront a production and delivery problem. I have watched a number of highly competent technical people quickly fail at new business ventures for one or several of the reasons given above. They gave little thought to areas other than technology and did not plan. Several cases will be discussed in Chapters 1, 2, and 6 to prove the point.

Starting and Managing a Small Business of Your Own presents a test for the would-be entrepreneur. Be honest with yourself when you take it. If you respond frankly and carefully review your answers, you can determine whether you are a real entrepreneur. If you are not, then I strongly recommend that you reconsider your plans to start up the new venture, because your chances of failure are much greater. I don't mean that all entrepreneurs are exactly alike—far from it. They tend to be very individualistic and they come from all walks of life. They do, however, share certain characteristics in common—and the SBA considers this to be of sufficient importance to put it first in its book, before discussing the details of how and when to get started.

In addition, psychological studies conducted by professionals have more to say on what the "typical" entrepreneur is like. These studies try to find patterns or similarities in early home life that mold and develop a person's attitudes. After interviewing a number of successful entrepreneurs, researchers found that successful entrepreneurs come from all levels of society, from the very rich to the very poor. Race, sex, color, age, religion, and natural origins did not seem to matter. They found that, in childhood, "the type" lived in a home in which the father was frequently absent and in which the mother was, therefore, the dominant influence.

The home life varied among those interviewed, but one common thread appeared: "the type" was given responsibility very early in life, and had to work things out alone. Entrepreneurs tended to be the oldest child, the one on whom the mother placed added responsibility to help her at home. They tended to get part-time jobs early on, and to have had regular duties at home as well. In cases in which one of the parents was ill and unable to perform typical parental duties, "the type" assumed some or all of those duties at a very early age.

Those who came from wealthier families may have been cared for by maids, nurses, and governesses during their early years and they may have been sent to boarding schools. They, too, received less than a typical amount of direct attention or care from the father. They had to think for and fend for themselves. They were not unhappy children, but they all recall hard work and family responsibility.

When I read this psychological analysis of the early life of the entrepreneur, I was amazed at how closely my own background conformed to it. I grew up during the Depression. My father was a fireman who worked 80 to 90 hours a week, and our family was organized around him not being there. After some years of part-time jobs and neighborhood chores, I had my first regular job at 12 years of age, and I've been working ever since. When we were both still in grammar school, my brother and I earned enough, between us, to pay the rent. We worked after school, on Saturdays, and during school vacations. It did make us grow up fast and caused us to assume adult attitudes and responsibilities at an early age.

Next, the psychologists noted that children who grew up to be entrepreneurs tended to be the organizers who managed or led school projects (plays, special projects, newspapers, debating clubs, and so on). Most of them were above-average students; few were top scholars. In general, they found school to be an enjoyable experience, but they had outside interests and were bored in the classroom if they saw no immediate and practical applications for their studies. However, they knew how to apply themselves and work hard and successfully in areas that they considered to be valuable and interesting.

If you are able to find some similarities between your own attitudes and those described by the SBA and by the psychological studies of entrepreneurs, then you'll have some indication of whether you are an entrepreneurial "type" or not.

The entrepreneur is also a *doer*. However, all doers are not entrepreneurs. An old management saying is that, in a typical organization, 90 percent of the work is done by 10 percent of the people. That 10 percent are the doers. They have great energy and good attitudes, they work hard and effectively, and they accomplish a great deal with little apparent effort. They are always ready to handle the unexpected and do not cave in. They rarely need pep talks or motivational lectures, but they can deliver those speeches to others. They are self-starters, and seem to be able to carry the load for others as well as for themselves.

In many business environments, the doers are taken advantage of by other workers. Invariably, doers are assigned the most work, the most difficult clients, or the most important projects. They are dependable, efficient, and thorough, and managers are confident that the job will be done, and done well, when a doer is assigned to the task. Unfortunately, when payday comes around the doer is not necessarily paid more than his less-productive peers. Like virtue, being a doer is its own reward. It is from this group of self-starters that successful entrepreneurs later emerge.

Are you a doer? You'll need to be one if you want to lead your own business venture. If you are unsure or uncertain as to whether or not you are a doer, then you aren't one. You shouldn't have to ask anyone else, you should know. And no one can make you into a doer if you aren't one by now.

The entrepreneur is the leader. He knows it's up to him to accomplish goals and to lead others to accomplish theirs. If you are not this type by nature, you are not very likely to succeed in any small business venture. It's best to accept the fact that you are what you are, and then find a suitable position in life. If your outlook on life or your nature is not suited to entrepreneurial activity, don't be upset. Everyone can't run a one-man business. That would be absurd, and would never work out. There's a place for everyone, and it's up to each of us to find our own.

I realize now that I have always been entrepreneurial in outlook and behavior. As a young man I was not aware of that, which led to some unhappy times. I didn't view my job the same way that many of my co-workers viewed theirs. That upset me and caused a great deal of soul-searching—until I realized what I was and did something about it.

At the age of 35, when most of us do some real thinking about where we are in life and what we want to be, I realized I did not like what I was doing. I was fairly successful as a middle-level manager in a large electronics company. I was a technical manager and was responsible for a department of 50 people. The department ran smoothly and I was often free to do other things. In discussing this with my superiors, I found they had few future plans, and, as long as my work was done on time and within budget, they felt I was doing very well. When I inquired about additional activities, I was told to "cool it." In fact, I was told I was too ambitious and was given a warning: "Don't rock the boat."

I gave some serious thought to going out on my own, but I didn't know anything about starting up a small business. So I visited the SBA office in Boston several times, and was given some very good advice. I was told that technical expertise is just one factor for success in a small business venture. I was advised to go to school, get an MBA degree, and then give it a try. I went to school for three years, in the evenings, got my MBA, and then felt I was ready. Two people whom I knew and respected joined me in the venture. We landed our first contract, and at 40 years of age I resigned from the large company and entered the entrepreneurial world. It is much different from any other job I have ever had, but it's my type of work. I have met other people who are or were operating a small business. Many failed because they were not suited to that type of work. Others have succeeded—or at least survived so far. Once again, in my judgment, the reasons for failure of those who went under were their attitudes and viewpoints.

The most common cause of failure early on was the tendency to remain strictly technical. For example, a friend of mine who has a Ph.D. in electrical engineering is a brilliant technical man. He and another Ph.D. landed one contract and started up a company. When that project drew to a close, he came to see me. We were about one year ahead of him in business and we had 18 people working for us. He asked me what the "trick" was. He thought I had some magic secret that he was unaware of. However, the "secret" of our success involved no magic. We marketed and sold our product enthusiastically. My friend had no knowledge of or interest in business techniques. He considered marketing and selling to be below him, and he never went out looking for new work because it embarrassed him to do so. I told him he would have to go out and market and sell himself and his company. Instead, he went back to his old job and let his plans and dreams and small venture end.

Another friend developed, in his own garage and with his own money, a remote terminal automatic plotting device. At the time (about 9 or 10 years ago), his device was a technological breakthrough. He asked me what he should do. He knew it was something new and innovative that had a large potential market. I asked if he had any sales or marketing plan. He said no and, further, said he knew of no way to sell it. The last I heard of him, he is working in Washington. I don't know what happened to his device.

About 10 years ago, one of our clients was a small manufacturing company. We were doing its payroll on our computer. The fellow who was handling the job for our company came to see me and said he had a problem. Our computer program sorted on names, and in this company 17 of 35 people had the same last name. (It was also the name of the company.) We changed the program to sort by Social Security number, which is what we should have done in the first place.

Clearly, here was a company in which nepotism had gotten completely out of hand. If half of the employees were related to each other, it's hard to imagine how the work was done, if it was done at all. Within six months the company was out of business and owed us for three months service (we never collected).

I mention this situation here because it is not a rare occurrence at all, and the odds against success increase if you include relatives and close friends in the new venture. No matter how much you love your relatives, nepotism has no place in the small venture.

Let's discuss the statistics of new business ventures. SBA statistics indicate that the majority fail within the first 12 to 24 months. Approximately 60 to 70 percent don't survive 18 months. Within five years, over 90 percent of small ventures are gone.

Another situation that merits attention concerns the young or middle-aged person who is entrepreneurial by nature and background, but who is working in a large bureaucratic environment in which entrepreneurial activity is discouraged or even punished. Entrepreneurs and bureaucrats are different, and entrepreneurs do not fit into a bureaucratic management environment. Sometimes they don't understand why and don't know what to do about it, but management in a bureaucratic environment is very different from management in an entrepreneurial environment. Let's discuss why they are different, and the serious problems that can arise when you mix them.

The bureaurcratic manager (BM) exists at all levels of every large organization. He or she can be responsible for anywhere from several people to up to tens of thousands of people. The function of the BM is to interpret and execute orders, policies, rules, and regulations as set forth by some higher authority. The rules are usually written down in a big book, and the BM knows where this book is and how to use it. He tries to apply the rules fairly and impartially in order to get the job done, keep morale high, keep employee turnover low, and keep complaints to a minimum. BMs hate controversy and change because they upset the normal routine. There is little opportunity for individualistic performance.

BMs seem to talk and act the same way as one another. They tend to dress alike and associate with each other. Sameness is desirable, and the replacement of one BM by another seems to have little or no effect on subordinates or on the way duties are discharged. Forms, procedures, and activities are set up to operate independently from the BM, whose job it is to see that things don't change. BMs are valuable to large organizations in which individuals who do things in a separate or distinctive way can create confusion. In those organizations, conscientious mediocrity is not only acceptable, it is preferable. Brilliant performers tend to try to improve or change things, and change is not a desirable factor within the bureaucracy. Established patterns and systems are what make the whole complex structure function and stay alive.

Here are a few examples of everyday situations that characterize the typical bureaucracy.

○ A BM is talking to a newly hired subordinate, who is an outstanding performer, and says that the person richly deserves a raise. However, the BM adds that company policy will not allow a raise for new employees until one year after arrival, no matter how good they are.

○ The BM knows that Mary outperforms all others in her group, but she gets the same percent increase as everyone else. In order to award Mary the raise she deserves, the BM would have had to send a special memorandum up through the chain of command, and he might have been turned down. He also knows that if Mary gets a bigger raise than the others, it could create morale problems and increase the turnover in the group.

○ The BM seems very concerned about how his group appears to others. A preoccupation with outward appearance (form) seems to be more important than actual performance (content). BMs often say, "It won't look good, if we do it that way," or "What will people think?"

○ You go to a BM with a problem or unusual situation that requires attention. He turns to the company's *Policies and Procedures Manual.* If the situation at hand is covered in the manual, the BM reads you the appropriate section, including the action (if any) to be taken. The BM then closes the manual, explains to you again what was written, and the discussion is closed. At times like this, you often hear BMs say things like, "I'd like to help you, but my hands are tied. I can't do anything except follow the manual in this case."

o "We can't do that, it's never been done before." This is another common statement that one hears in a bureaucratic environment. BMs are very wary of innovative or new techniques. They assume there will be little reward if the new technique should work out but there's plenty to lose if it doesn't, so why take the risk?

o When something goes wrong, it takes the BM far too long to straighten it out. A BM tends to write reports about a problem instead of solving it. This is sometimes called "diaper management." You cover your own bottom first, before you try to remedy the situation. That's like firemen trying to determine how the fire started before they begin putting out the flames.

o BMs form and participate in many committees and coordination meetings. At one former place of employment, I found I was required to attend coordination meetings that took up between 15 to 25 hours of my time each week. Later on I began sending my section managers to these meetings and committees. I told them it was to introduce them to the higher levels of internal company management, but the real reason was that I didn't want to attend them. In my opinion, most of the meetings were a costly waste of time.

You might, by this time, conclude that I am hostile toward BMs. However, that is not the case. I believe that under certain circumstances, BMs have an important role to play and can make a valuable contribution.

Let us now discuss the entrepreneurial manager (EM). The EM is the antithesis of the BM in almost every respect. The EM generally works in an unstructured or rapidly changing environment in which policies and procedures are out of date as soon as or before they are written. Routine, sameness, orderliness, and predictability are not part of the EM's world. If we consider an hourglass, and take the narrow part through which the sand passes as the manager's responsibility, then the BM takes the job and looks downward into the lower half and makes sure the sand goes through in an orderly, measurable, and predictable way. However, the EM looks upward to the sand that has not yet passed through the narrow opening and wonders where it comes from, why it is sand and not some other substance, whether he has to use an hourglass at all, and who looks at the hourglass and why. The EM looks upward and outward; the BM looks inward and downward. These different outlooks result in different managerial approaches.

Here are some typical comments and attitudes exhibited by and about the EM in his environment:

○ The EM hired a new employee six months ago. Today he doubled that employee's salary because the new person contributed a bright new idea.

○ There are no published organization charts. No one seems to know who is in charge of whom and why. There are no fixed policies.

○ Nobody seems to be very worried about budgets, schedules, costs, and so on. (They are concerned, but that's not apparent at first.)

○ People are informal. Even low-level people call the EM by his first name.

○ The EM seems to never know what time it is; once he gets going it's impossible to stop him. EMs work on into the night. Time has little meaning to them.

○ EMs seem to jump from one project to another. They don't work for years on one long-term project. They get bored easily when things become routine.

○ EMs like to change things—sometimes, it seems, for no good reason other than love of change itself.

○ Over the weekend, the EM reorganized the division and on Monday everyone got new assignments.

○ EMs act on impulse and intuition rather than by carefully analyzing and studying a situation. Sometimes they move too fast and without sufficient justification. They take many risks.

EMs and BMs function, think, and act in very different ways. Neither is entirely right or entirely wrong. It all depends on what the job is, how you want it done, and what method you want to use to reach the desired goal. EMs tend to be associated with R&D jobs, new technologies, educational institutions, new business ventures, large new projects, and creative and innovative enterprises.

There is a place for the EM in big corporations. There has to be or those organizations wouldn't survive or grow. The problem is that EMs are often very high up in their organizations, and most of the people working in middle management or below rarely come in contact with them. A young or budding EM is not very likely to find his attitude and behavior pattern appreciated or even understood by a BM who, very likely, is his immediate supervisor. You generally get very little encouragement for entrepreneurial activities in a big company. You have to generate your own initiative and drive, and then defend or explain it to some superior, who very likely doesn't understand what you are trying to do or why, and who may even put you down as a troublemaker.

BMs find homes mostly in large government and commercial operations, in business areas of educational institutions, or on large, ongoing projects. Each has a place in the scheme of things and, generally, there are far more BMs than EMs. Trouble of major proportions usually arises when a BM is assigned to a task that calls for an EM, or when an EM is assigned to a task for which a BM would be better suited.

For example, the manager of a small business was hired by a large computer software group. He had been on the job a few months and was doing a good job, after working hard to get settled in. He entered the computer room one day and saw punched-paper output tape from the computers falling on the floor and being walked on by the people using the computer. He went to a supply house, purchased several tape reels with his own money, and put the paper tapes on the tape reels so that they would no longer get walked on and ruined. He was not reimbursed for the price of the tape reels (he did not fill out the required requisition form and forward it to purchasing) and he received a dressing down from his boss for interfering in the operations of another department. The manager of the computer room had complained, in writing, about the new manager's attitude and interference. Several weeks later the new manager left for lunch and never returned.

A manager at another large corporation tried to use new software techniques to automate the drafting department, improve efficiency, and reduce costs. He was openly and immediately rebuffed by the manager of the drafting department, who never spoke to him again. Also, he was told by his own boss to stay within his area of responsibility, and not to disturb any other areas in the division. This man left the company shortly thereafter and set up his own small business.

The president of a small company awaited the arrival of a new senior staff member with pleasure and anticipation. The honeymoon ended quickly; the new person seemed slow and rigid, and was unresponsive to the changing environment. He was always looking for rules and guidelines to follow. He would not make the necessary decisions and spent more time writing reports to the company president about problems than he did in solving the problems. The new employee had worked in large, structured companies for many years. Despite many attempts to convince him that the procedures of a big company were not always applicable in the environment of a small company, he was unable to understand or accept this. As a result, after six unhappy months of trying to adjust he left the small business and returned to the formal, structured environment of the bureaucracy. He had this to say about bureaucratic managers: "They always knew what they were doing, how to do it, and where responsibility started and stopped."

When a small business suddenly expanded, a newly hired person was made manager of a new department. He had trouble recruiting new people to add to his staff, and after a few months, senior managers got directly involved in the situation. They discovered that the new manager had simply refused to hire many qualified applicants because their salary requirements were higher than the wages paid for comparable people at his former place of employment. He was even using the wage guidelines of his old company as his sole guide to entrance salaries. When he was told that this small business had no guidelines, that each new person was evaluated on the basis of his own individual merits and experience, plus company needs, he became very upset—such practices were inefficient, and resulted in unfair variances among salaries. He was aghast to learn that promotions and raises were based on performance alone, not on time in the job. Shortly afterward, he resigned.

It should be clear by now that some positions are suited to EMs, and others are right for BMs. There is a role for each, and rightly so. It is not a good idea for an EM to work as a bank manager in charge of loans. He would not follow the rules. He might play hunches, and would probably violate banking laws in doing so. A BM who religiously follows the rules, formulas, and procedures is the person for that job. But a BM would be a catastrophe working in a research company or in a new business environment, in which there are no rules to follow and conditions change by the hour. He would be unable to make decisions, to stop a project or start a new effort, to commit funds, or to take risks in unknown or uncertain areas.

If you are an EM in a BM environment, I suggest you carefully rethink your situation now and take the necessary corrective action as soon as you can. Otherwise, you may blame yourself for not being as happy and contented as everyone else. It's up to you to do what has to be done—the BMs you work with will be confused by your behavior but won't know how to rectify the situation. However, if a BM is in an EM environment, that situation will correct itself very quickly. An EM will quickly sense that the BM is like a fish out of water.

People work at their jobs for a variety of reasons, but the factors high on just about everyone's list are job satisfaction, a sense of value, personal satisfaction, and the knowledge that a contribution is being made. EMs and BMs both matter. They both make contributions, each in his own way. Job satisfaction is as important as and in many ways more important than the salary earned. Since it's your life and you get only one shot, it is important to determine which type of manager you are and want to be, and to act accordingly.

In general, fewer EMs are required in any operation. Sooner or later, the successful, growing, and profitable business requires policies, procedures, rules, regulations, and a settled and predictable environment. An EM can inhibit the continued success of a successful enterprise if he maintains his entrepreneurial methods after they have ceased to be effective. If you consider a company to be like a play, the EM is analogous to the first act. It has to be good or you won't stay for the remaining acts. The BMs correspond to the second and third acts of the play. They stay the longest, eventually do most of the work, and, unfortunately for the EMs, tend to get most of the rewards in the long term.

In a small business, one entrepreneur is generally enough at the start. The old saying that "too many cooks spoil the broth" applies here. Just as not having an entrepreneur in the enterprise can cause trouble and eventual failure, having two or more entrepreneurs at the same level of a small business can work at cross-purposes and be counterproductive. They may argue, protest, and disagree over courses of action, prices, delivery times, and so on.

For several years our company had serious problems. Two of us were entrepreneurs and we clashed loudly and often over many business matters. It came very near to breaking up the company, but we both realized the value of making the company come first and not letting our differences get out of hand.

We have discussed at some length the entrepreneur: what he is like, why he is vital to any new business venture, what can and does happen when new businesses are formed by people who are not entrepreneurs. Entrepreneurs are vital to the success of any business venture and, if you cannot clearly identify yourself as the entrepreneurial type, then you should avoid putting yourself in a business situation that requires an entrepreneur. The risk of failure is too high, and even if you succeed initially, the personal price of trying to be something that you are not may not be worth it.

If you have been dissuaded from starting a new venture by reading this, then you probably wouldn't have succeeded. Nothing can stop the real entrepreneur. No written reports or risks of failure will ever prevent him from giving it a try (sometimes over and over again). If you can now honestly say to yourself that you *are* the type, that's great! The rest of this book discusses the situations that you may encounter, describes the pitfalls that await you, and looks at how others have fared.

If you are not the type, reading this may help you better understand the entrepreneur—how he views his business and does his job. Many large organizations and government agencies deal with small businesses through subcontracting. If the managers of large organizations can more fully understand and appreciate the small business environment and the entrepreneurs, they can reap greater rewards from their business dealings with small subcontractors.

My company does a great deal of business with the U.S. government, and the regulations require that each fiscal year our books and records be audited in detail, by the federal audit agency. Each year, a team of government auditors comes out to visit us and spends days or weeks with our accountant and a consulting firm to approve our rates, prices, profit, and so on. We don't like it, but we have to submit to this annual interrogation if we want to do business with the government. Recently, the leader of the government audit team told me that he and his associates had, over the years, watched our company grow. The auditor said that they just didn't understand how we operated with sudden and drastic changes in policies and personnel, changes in work and changes of clients.

To him and his associates, changes indicated trouble, not improvement. However, profit was a foreign concept to his group. I told him that this was the basic difference between a bureaucratic and an entrepreneurial organization. Because of the place they work, the job they do, and what they want from their careers, that auditor and his associates may never understand our approach. Having worked for the government earlier in my career, I was able to appreciate how they viewed their jobs and how they viewed us. In his working environment, success comes with the pension one receives as retirement.

In short, we work with risk, and the government people—with their tenure and job security—do not. We win or lose on every job we do. Yes indeed, the two types of jobs are very different. Entrepreneurs are aware of the difference. They have to be, or they wouldn't survive very long.

This book is not intended to be "The Saga of Bill Delaney." It is intended for those who want to learn about some typical problems and pitfalls that beset the entrepreneur in his small business venture. The examples are drawn from my own experiences and mistakes, and from the experiences of people who have told me what has happened to them. It is hoped that you will be able to use that information to your advantage if you find yourself in similar situations.

2

Defining Your Goals and Making Your Plans

"The end in view is a true cause." This philosophical quote simply means that the ultimate reason for any activity should be the true cause of everything that happens. For example, in a football game the primary end in view is to win games by scoring points and by preventing the other team from scoring. Thus, the team's activities, such as recruiting, practices, extra coaching, and viewing game films, are directed first toward scoring touchdowns and then toward preventing the other team from scoring. Field goals and safeties are lower on the list. If a coach became so preoccupied with field goals that he directed his primary training activities and efforts in that direction, he wouldn't last long, because his team wouldn't have a successful season.

A person may start his own business venture for many reasons:

1. To have the freedom to do things his way.
2. To be his own boss.
3. To make more money.
4. To get out from under and start over.

5. To live and work in a different environment.
6. To provide a special new product or service not now in existence.

You may have other good reasons for wanting to start up your own business venture. Whatever the reasons, a very good first step is to write them all down, think about them, and arrange them according to importance. You'll probably have several reasons for wanting to go on your own; you had better decide what your priorities are, because you can't accomplish all your goals simultaneously. What comes first? If the priorities conflict, what is deferred or deleted? I can assure you that no matter how deeply and how long you think about your basic plan, there will be something that you will forget or be unable to anticipate. An old military maxim is, "No plan survives the shock of battle." However, it's better to enter the fray with some plan in mind than to start the affair with no clear goals. A goal is, at least, a reference point by which you can gauge your progress. Can you imagine a football game in which no score is kept? As silly as this sounds, some people do start up new business ventures with no clear idea of what their goal is. They sort of ease into it, one step at a time, until they are fully committed—with no clearly defined goal.

It is important for you to think long and carefully about what you want to achieve from your new business venture. Gather information from any sources that you can, including the following:

1. The Small Business Administration.
2. Local business schools.
3. Special consultants.
4. Successful small business entrepreneurs.
5. Your congressman and senator.
6. The "old boy" network.
7. Private small business organizations.

The SBA was discussed at length in Chapter 1. Its value as a source of information, guidance, and assistance cannot be over-emphasized.

Many people are not aware that local business schools and colleges are a source of free assistance. The business school faculty, in many cases, is ready and willing to spend time with you and give you access to information, advice, and guidance that you could not buy at any price. Although teachers will be more than willing to talk to you and help you in any way they can, don't make a nuisance of yourself by visiting them repeatedly and taking up a great deal of their time. Visit once, for an hour or so. After that, you can call them, now and then, for answers to specific questions or to request specific advice. Remember, it's not quantity that counts in this situation. It's the quality of the information you receive—and I know of no one who could give you higher quality information than the professors in any good business school. You will probably find that if a professor can't talk to you himself, he'll refer you to a colleague who specializes in your area of interest.

Some years ago, I read a newspaper article about a young couple on their way to start a new life in California. Their truck broke down in a small town in New Mexico, and they had to stay there and get jobs in order to save up enough money to repair the truck. One Sunday morning, the fellow read a newspaper article about people who were prospecting for uranium in the hills around where they were staying. He became interested. He went to the state university and asked to speak to the head of the geology department. He asked the professor where the best area to search for uranium would be. The professor went over to a map on his office wall and pointed to a location that was a two-hour drive from the campus. The young fellow noted the location, bought a Geiger counter, and drove to that spot. The Geiger counter went off the scale. He staked his claim and became a wealthy man. You may wonder why the professor never went out to see for himself. Frankly, I don't know, but that's typical. Professors can and will advise others, but rarely take action themselves. However, the information they provide may be just what you need. So take advantage of this very useful source of guidance.

Special consultants can be very useful as well, but they generally cost money that the new entrepreneur cannot afford. Also, some consultants will mislead inexperienced entrepreneurs simply to earn a fat fee without being helpful. As in any other business, the majority are honest, well-intentioned people who can be of assistance. Before you pay for consultants, I recommend that you know exactly what you want from them and that you use a large, established consulting firm. You are more likely to get the information you need that way than if you use a one-man operation, which may not have the expertise that you require. Also, the larger consulting firms have their reputations to consider, so you're much less likely to be led astray, even though they are a bit more expensive. Once again, it's the quality of the information you are after at this stage, not the amount of time you'll spend with the consultant. One hour with the right person is preferable to 20 hours with the wrong one. Early on in our business I used several one-man operations as consultants, and in only one case did it work out. I advise caution at this stage. When funds are limited, you can't afford a mistake.

You may think that people who have successfully started a small business would not be likely to help you, but many are only too happy to assist you. As long as you won't adversely affect their business or become a competitor, many will take the time and trouble to give you a great deal of good business information.

They remember how difficult it was for them at the beginning, when they were struggling. As a result, successful entrepreneurs will gladly guide you through the mine fields of state and local taxes, insurance, sources of customers, basic accounting, pricing, selling techniques, and so on. You will be very pleasantly surprised to find out how willing they are to help you. It's almost like meeting a fraternity brother or sorority sister.

You can get a great deal of useful information from your congressmen and senators by simply writing to them and requesting it. They have large staffs in Washington and in their home offices for just that purpose. I called my congressman's local office and got an appointment to see him. He was very congenial and set up an appointment for me with one of his aides in Washington, who could help me get information on how to apply for government contracts. The aide not only gave me a list as long as my arm, he spent the entire day with me and he took me to many of the major government agencies that issue contracts for government supplies and services. I would never have been able to uncover this source of potential business any other way. (We did get a contract from one of the sources he made known to me.) It's to everyone's benefit if your new venture succeeds. Your congressman or senator wants a prosperous constituency at home. The more work you get, the more people you'll hire. If more people are working, more taxes are being paid, so everyone benefits. Your congressman can also be influential in getting security clearance for you, which will allow you to bid on classified proposals. Don't overlook this excellent source of help and guidance. It's free and can be very useful.

The "old boy" network is alive and well. Use it! I'm sure that during your career, you have helped others in some way and done favors for friends at work. If so, collect on your IOUs. Ask those people for any aid and assistance you need. Many of them will be only too glad to help out. Later on they may need your assistance. This network can be very useful for getting new business, recruiting personnel, and locating banks and other institutions that may be sources of capital. I recommend that you sit down in a quiet place, review a list of all the people in business whom you know, consider how many of them can be of assistance to you, and act accordingly.

Finally, there are many good small business associations that you can join, usually for a very reasonable fee. As a member, you can get group insurance at very low rates, receive information in areas of interest to small business, and get leads on new clients.

You also get a chance to meet and know your fellow entrepreneurs, who can help you get started. You can, in some cases, gain access to legal and financial advisers and institutions that you would not otherwise be aware of.

I strongly suggest that you use any or all of these potential sources of aid before you start up your enterprise—not after—because you will need most of your help right at the start. The first six months are critical. You may not have time to pursue certain avenues if you wait until you find you need specific assistance, so check these sources out early.

Now, define your reason for starting your new venture. Be specific. If you have several goals, list them in order of importance. If you can't write your goal down, or if it is vague or imprecise, then you won't be able to make a specific plan. There are many ways to plan a trip, but you can't begin to do so until you know your destination and know when you want to get there.

After you have clearly defined what you want to achieve in your new venture, you'll need to plan how to achieve it and by when. Once again, your plan should be written down and should be carefully reviewed and re-examined before you start on your new business venture. Generally, you should make a five-year plan, a one-year plan, and a three-month plan. It is not an easy thing to do, but it can be done. Identify at least one check point per month (but no more than one per week) so you can gauge your progress, as you would on any long trip. It is interesting and alarming to read that the majority of small business entrepreneurs cannot understand a profit-and-loss statement or a balance sheet. Since these are two of the most important and basic documents in any business, being ignorant of them can and will cause serious business problems for the new entrepreneur. If a person tried to be a lawyer without understanding how juries function, how successful do you think he'd be? Lawyers must pass rigorous examinations so such things are not going to happen. There are no examinations or tests required for anyone who wants to start up a new business. As a result, the alarming situation described above is real. This is, in my opinion, one of the major reasons why so many small businesses fail so quickly. Because they have no plan, no pro forma P&L statements, and no balance sheets against which they can compare actual performance, would-be entrepreneurs confuse growth with profit. Many suddenly find that, in spite of a booming and expanding new business, they are out of cash. Often, it all ends before they even knew what happened.

In 1965, when we started our business, we made a very detailed five-year plan. In 1970, we were off by 9 percent on the high side. We aren't geniuses, so planning for success doesn't require superhuman effort. Your plan should be flexible enough that you can react to real events as they occur and can adjust your actions and possibly change course if necessary. Consider the case of a fellow who ran a small fish store. On his trips to Boston to buy fresh fish, he started picking up "trash fish" for his customers to give to their cats. At first he gave the fish away. His business improved, so he started to charge a small amount to cover his costs and transportation. The business continued to grow. He found he was selling more fish for cats than for people, so he went into the cat-food business. Now he is one of the largest cat-food producers in the country, and has no more fish stores. He reacted to an unforeseen opportunity. I use this example to point out that along the way you may see a golden opportunity in an entirely new area that you had not considered in your original plan. Do not stick religiously to any plan, if you can see opportunities in other, unanticipated areas. Make a new plan, adjust and redefine it to reflect the real situation, and go on from there.

You might even rethink your original goals, at that point, and determine if they need revision. If your goal was strictly financial, it doesn't much matter what type of business you are in to reach it (but you may have to redefine your charter if you are incorporated). In any case, don't forget to re-examine your basic company goal every six months or so.

Now you must decide the type of business structure you want to have. Do you want a proprietorship, partnership, or corporation? There are advantages and disadvantages to each one. Which is best for you depends on what your goals and plans are. This is discussed in Chapter 5.

Next you must consider when to make your move. Starting a new venture at the onset of a recession can end it all before the year is out. Timing is important, so give it full and careful consideration. (See Chapter 5.) The bankruptcy courts are full of companies who started at the wrong time or in the wrong place. Let me give you some examples.

As incredible as this is going to seem, I know of a fellow who started a business as a landscape gardener in New England in November. He was out of business by April of the following year. I asked him if he was next going to start a snow plowing business in July, but he didn't see the humor of my remark.

A couple I also know planned to open a resort motel at the beach in June. They encountered the construction delays and initial problems that are all part of the game, but that they had not counted on. By September everything was finally set. They signed the papers, released the payments to the contractors, and incurred a large bank mortgage that required heavy monthly payments. From October until the following May the couple had a steady outgoing cash flow of fixed charges, taxes, heating bills, maintenance, and mortgage. They were reeling by May, and it all could have been avoided by simply not accepting the completed motel until the start of the next tourist season, when the income from tourists would help meet these costs. I asked them later why they took possession so soon. The reply they gave me was very human, but most unbusinesslike. They said they had wanted to own a motel for so long that they couldn't wait to take possession and move in. Don't let your heart rule your head in the business world. It's a very dangerous thing to do.

There is one final item that merits discussion in this chapter on

advance planning. Plan for success and growth. Before you conclude that I have just made a ridiculous statment, let me advise you
that many companies fail because they don't plan for success. One
of the many ways to plan any future activity is to plot three curves.
First plot the curve of what you really expect to happen. Then plan
and work toward that goal. Next, plot the most optimistic growth
curve that you can imagine. This one has a low but finite probabil-
ity of occurrence. (Never plan or act on possibilities, because something may be possible but very unlikely. Keep your planning real-
istic.) Finally, take the most pessimistic outlook and plot the lowest
level of business activity that you can tolerate without having to
throw in the towel. Now you have three growth curves on your
graph. What you expect and are planning for has an 85 to 90 percent chance of falling somewhere in between the top or bottom line
on the graph. By carefully monitoring your progress each month,
you can see where your actual business activity falls.

I suggest that you give some thought to unexpected good fortune or early success because most people don't consider this option or they don't plan for it. I observed, in a very large corporation, the deep depression, gloom, and almost panic that set in after
a group was advised that it had won a very large government contract. The managers had not considered it very likely that they
would win the job, and their staffs were fully committed to other
projects. Any weekend poker player can tell you that when you're
winning big and you bet on and draw for an inside straight, you will
usually win. But when you're losing and borrow to bet heavily on
four aces, the other fellow will come up with a royal flush. But business ventures are not like poker games. I have seen several new
companies grow beyond their wildest dreams and, in attempting to
take on more and more work, take on uncoordinated short- and
long-term loans to finance the unexpected and unplanned new
business. When the notes were called in and they couldn't borrow
any more funds, they went bankrupt. Rapid growth does not automatically mean more profit. Plot your three curves, and for a few

years stay within them. Then plan and plot new projections. Don't try to grow too fast. Rapid growth has killed off many a good venture early on.

I fully appreciate how difficult it is to turn away unexpected new business. I have done it, and it hurts. But you must exert discipline on yourself and on your company. Growing in a steady, planned, and orderly fashion is preferable to bursting on the scene like a sky-rocket, soaring high in the heavens, and then falling to earth as a burned-out shell. It's better to be a small satellite, climb into the sky slowly, and stay in orbit indefinitely.

If you want to be around for the long run, you must make your own business objectives and follow your own plans to achieve them in an orderly way. Disordered growth in the human or corporate body is cancer, and is just as deadly in either case.

3

Choosing Your Partners

The title of this chapter sounds like an invitation to a dance. Unfortunately, in business it is not that easy. A business partner or associate, once chosen, cannot be as easily set aside as a dance partner is when the music stops. He becomes part of your venture for better or worse. Howard Hughes is reported to have said that his father had advised him to never take on a business partner, as they are generally more trouble than they are worth. A very experienced businessman told me that having business partners is like getting married, because, if you or they want to separate or break off the relationship later on, it is not an easy thing to do. The person who is invited to leave often does not want to, and may fight back to protect his "rights."

There are three basic forms that any new venture can take: the proprietorship, the partnership, and the corporation. These are discussed in detail in Chapter 5, but they merit a brief discussion here because the form of your venture greatly affects the importance of business partners or associates.

If you have a proprietorship, then you own it all and you are the sole boss. There's no question: it's yours and yours alone. No matter how many people work for you, they can only suggest or recommend what they want to do or how it is to be done. As the sole proprietor, you call the shots. You don't have to worry about what others think about what you do. You issue the orders or you do it yourself, your own way.

There are strengths and weaknesses in this sort of venture. If it is small and stays small, then it is possible for one person to do it all—keep the books, run the store, supervise several employees—and still be very efficient. This is the strength of the proprietorship. Now, what are the weaknesses? It cannot grow very fast, because one person can't handle a larger business.

For example, if the proprietor is a TV repairman or the owner and operator of a laundromat or a gasoline service station, he may know a great deal about washing machines or automobiles, but little or nothing about business and legal procedures. He may inadvertently break some state or federal law. In choosing the proprietorship form for your new venture, you may be limiting your opportunities for growth and expansion, either because you are too busy to be aware of other growth opportunities or because you don't have the staff to take on the new work.

In general, if you initiate a new venture then you want and (hopefully) are planning for growth and expansion. Sooner or later you will take on partners or choose associates, and form either a partnership or a corporation. (The advantages and disadvantages of these two forms of business are discussed in Chapter 5.) In either case, you have to select and bring in part owners who have a piece of your business venture. Even if you don't want to do this, it may be necessary in many situations. Here are some typical reasons why you may offer people an ownership position in your new venture:

1. You may require the services of a senior person, whose talents and experience are vital to your expansion. In such cases,

good people are usually employed elsewhere. You have to attract them to join your venture, and you have to retain their interest. Offering a part ownership in the new venture can induce some to join you if they can't get such an opportunity anywhere else.

2. At the start, you may not be able to afford the high salaries that the people you want can get elsewhere. Sometimes, they will take a lower initial salary if stock or some other partial ownership plan is part of the deal.

3. If your new venture is heavily dependent upon people with special skills or talents (computer programmers, accountants, or lawyers) whose personal presence or absence can cause you to gain or lose clients, you may have to offer them part ownership to retain their interest or to prevent them from leaving and going into competition with you.

4. If there is typically a high employee turnover in the type of business you are in, one way to reduce this turnover is to offer company stock as part of an ownership plan to employees.

5. You may need a loan to finance expansion or to use as working capital as your company grows. In such cases, it is not at all unusual that the lending agency demands the opportunity to buy into your company at their discretion at some point in the future. For example, if you borrow $1 million and you plan to repay it in two or three years at a given rate of interest, the lending agency may require that they have the option, at the time of repayment, to receive either the $1 million and accrued interest or a certain amount of stock in your enterprise (at a predetermined price). This gives the lending agency the option to get their money back or to choose your stock. Naturally, they won't choose your stock unless it is worth far more than the price of the loan plus the interest. If you need the money, you may have no choice but to accept these terms.

There are many other reasons for acquiring business partners or close associates, but you should try to keep this sort of thing to a minimum, as Howard Hughes did during his career. Admittedly, few of us are as successful as Howard Hughes, but it does not hurt to listen to, learn about, and try to emulate those things that he did—or any successful person does.

Once again, before you start thinking about awarding shares or making people part owner of your new venture, get competent legal and accounting advice from an objective source. The bigger law firms, banks, or accounting firms are your best bet. If your legal or CPA advisers have a special interest in your company because of a share in ownership, this may work out exactly opposite to what you had in mind. They may put their small interest first and advise counter to the overall best interests of your business. For example, if you have several people who have a small share in your venture and you plan to bring others into the venture to gain special expertise for additional growth, it is not unusual for you to receive a negative reaction from the current stockholders. They may be afraid that issuing more and more stock will dilute their share of ownership and reduce the potential value of their shares. In such cases, you may not get an objective evaluation of your future business plans.

I can speak from personal experience in this situation. It took me several years to figure out why a person who was intelligent, aggressive, and a risk-taker when he worked for a large commercial company became a conservative, negative, and fearful employee after he joined our firm, with a piece of the ownership as an incentive. He was so overly concerned about his shares losing value that he no longer functioned effectively. Other unfortunate things can occur after you choose your partners or issue stock to employees. These are discussed below.

Instead of working harder and showing more interest in the success and growth of the new venture, employees may actually slack off. They may believe that as part owners they can come or go as they please. Some may refuse assignments that they don't want to do or focus on work that should be phased out.

Some people react in exactly an opposite fashion. They become too interested and involved in corporate operations, financial transactions, and other high-level interests, and consequently spend less and less time doing their assigned tasks. And why not? They own part of the business, so it is their right to be interested in what is going on at the corporate level each and every day. They can and will demand long and exact explanations to account for every penny earned or spent by the company. Sometimes, even spouses and other family members start calling up corporate executives to ask questions or demand explanations. The father of one of our employees called repeatedly to question company activities. He used to say that he was looking out for his boy's interests. The fact that his "boy" was 45 years old seemed not to matter. This can be a very unpleasant situation, and one that's difficult to avoid.

Success, sudden wealth, and unexpected good fortunes can change many people. Your hard-working scientists or business associates may lose interest in daily work when the stock they own becomes very valuable. They may want to start enjoying life right away.

Consider the person you brought into the company with a stock incentive who, as time goes on, becomes less and less effective. The employee didn't live up to expectations and, for the good of the company, must be fired. Now you have a problem. When he departs, his share in the new venture goes with him. He may sell it or he may hold it and let you go on earning money for him while he contributes nothing toward your goals.

A business acquaintance of mine had to buy back an interest in his own real estate venture from a departing employee, who was discharged for taking kickbacks from suppliers and passing the costs on to his own real estate company. It cost my acquaintance over $65,000 to buy back that employee's interest in the company. He thought the man would be valuable to his enterprise, but instead he turned out to be expensive.

As you can see, giving out shares or part interest in a new venture won't always elicit the response you expect. In many companies, people are willing to pitch in and work long hours for low pay when the company is starting out and has little capital. Later, however, these same people may demand fabulous raises and vastly excessive fringe benefits and perquisites when the company starts to prosper. In the early years at our company, executives emptied the wastepaper baskets and cleaned the floors after hours, because we could not afford a cleaning service. Some of these same people now wouldn't pick up a paperclip if they dropped one on the floor.

What happens if a person to whom you awarded stock or part ownership becomes ill or dies? This is difficult to deal with on a personal level, but you must also reassign work to others who may already have a full share. On top of all that, the person's spouse will want to know what you plan to do. This situation is discussed more fully in Chapter 5, but it is mentioned here because if the person had stock or was a part owner, the situation will be more complicated.

There are many ways to choose and reward business associates. The most important thing to keep in mind is that business partners should be chosen in the same way that porcupines kiss each other: very carefully. To avoid entirely the problems discussed above, maintain complete ownership. However, this is not always possible. You may not be able to get or keep all the talent you will need to expand and grow without some sort of stock option plan. In that case, keep in mind the following:

1. Don't give out stock or ownership interest up front. Let employees work for your company and demonstrate their value first.

2. Don't be too generous in your attempts to be fair. If employees don't ask for it, don't volunteer stocks or part ownership. Once given, financial interest can never be returned—you must buy it back.

3. Try other methods of added compensation first, such as bonuses, trips, fringe benefits, and perquisites. The people you want often find these incentives to be just as acceptable as stock options or part ownership.

4. Be very careful that you don't lose control of your own organization. This usually won't occur unless your venture becomes so successful and valuable that other parties are motivated to move against you.

5. Try to make any ownership arrangement contingent upon active and successful contribution toward the attainment of specific corporate goals, such as level of sales or profit.

If you have determined that I am suggesting that you be very careful and very conservative in the initial distribution of your stock or ownership, you are correct. I learned this the hard way, for I was overly generous in the initial distribution of shares. In our new business venture, I made most of the mistakes I have advised you to avoid, and have paid full price for every one of them. I hope you'll learn from my mistakes.

I distributed voting stock to several people at the start. One person later refused to work on assigned tasks and would not join our company. He sold us our own stock. Another person became ill for a year and a half and left the company, but later returned. A third person never worked out because of personality problems.

One entrepreneur gave up a majority interest in his new venture to get required initial funding. Several years later, when he had brought the company up to a very profitable level, he was replaced as the top person. Those who had a financial interest in the company voted to put one of their own in charge.

Please consider that the people you may need at the start may not be the same ones you will need later on. If you distributed an unnecessarily large portion of your stock early on, then you won't have enough available later to induce other managers and senior staff personnel to join your operation. In many respects, a new business venture is like a military operation. The entrepreneur and his first group are like the assault troops. Most are eliminated or injured in the early going when they have to break into a new business and breach the line of competitors to get a business toehold. This is the most difficult part of the business venture. That's why the casualty rate is so high for the first year or two. At times like this, one or two people can make or break the entire operation, because the fighting is fierce and progress is measured in small increments. Individual effort, at this stage, is very important. You work on a month-to-month or even a day-to-day basis until you break through and get a big contract. Then you can call up the reserve or support forces to capitalize on the opportunity and maximize profits.

As with a military operation, a business operation requires two different types of people: the "assault troops" and the "reserves." The person on the beach who is struggling to stay alive and perhaps gain another 200 yards in the face of fierce resistance cannot be expected to be thinking of the overall plan for the big advance. But somebody had better be thinking about it. Otherwise, no one will be there to capitalize on the opportunity, and all of the sacrifice to get to that point will have been wasted. As the entrepreneur, it's up to you to plan and direct it all. If you choose partners and associates who can help you for a year or two but are unable to help you exploit your hard-earned business position, all of your hard work, sacrifice, and effort will be wasted.

Hire as many people as you can who are capable of going a little way with you. Hold back on stock options. You certainly should allow them to buy stock at a bargain rate, if and when you go public. At that time, there will be so many owners that you may well be able to control the corporation by holding at most 30 or 40 percent of company stock.

If you are just starting out or have a growing but closely held corporation, then you can open yourself up to a great deal of needless aggravation and argument and can end up wasting your time and energy dealing with unhappy or unproductive employees who are also stockholders. They will demand your attention, not as subordinate employees, but as stockholders for whom you work. Some people are not able to separate their dual roles of employee and part owner in a company. Many people fully understand and appreciate the difference, but some do not. Those people will surely divert the entrepreneur from leading his venture. Instead of directing his full attention to the outside business world or new company business, the entrepreneur finds himself constantly pulled at from within his company by an unhappy employee/stockholder who has a never-ending series of questions and problems that are in no way connected with expansion, growth, or profit.

Just as in any other phase of life, if you use your own good judgment, plan ahead for the long run, and act in accordance with your plans, you should do well. If, however, you act too quickly and choose the wrong partners or shareholders, then you will pay the price. "Marry in haste and repent at leisure."

Of course, such situations are problems only if your venture is successful—15 or 30 percent of nothing is nothing. If you are as successful as you plan to be, do you really want one person or several people to own 15 or 30 percent of your business? Your annual sales may be $10 million or $20 million a year. Think about it now. Are those people really that important to you and what you plan to do? The money to which they will be legally, ethically, and morally entitled may be far in excess of the contributions they made to your organization.

In an advice column in the newspaper, a young fellow described the following experience. He bought two tickets (for 50¢ each) on a $1,000 door prize. He gave one to his girl friend, who later won the $1,000 drawing. She never mentioned it to him again. He felt she should share the prize with him but she told him to "take a walk." The boy asked the columnist if he had a legal right to share the $1,000. The answer was that he had no right, legally, to any portion of the $1,000, because he gave his girl friend the ticket and she owned it. But the columnist added that the girl had no class. She should have shared the money with her boy friend, but she chose not to do so. The boy was advised that he had learned a good lesson and for only 50¢. If the event had not occurred, he might have married the young lady, and would be paying a far greater price.

Anyone who studies and analyzes small business statistics has read that the primary reason for failure is mistakes by management. I suppose that is true, but there are many kinds of mistakes you can make. The statement that mismanagement is the cause of failure is too simplistic. That's the same as saying that the primary cause of divorce is marital problems. That's true, but not very informative. One has to try to find out what the proximate causes are for the mismanagement or for the marital problems.

In business, problems with partners, stockholders, or part owners have caused the premature demise of more new ventures than any statistical report indicates. Internal bickering and arguments and the resulting inefficiencies do not show directly as a corporate liability on any P&L statement or balance sheet the way that "good will" is listed as an asset. The results of internal bickering shows up as a decrease in sales, a decline in profit, and an increase in costs. In such cases, an analysis of the books and records would lead one to conclude that corporate failure was caused by a reduction in sales, followed by departure of key personnel, followed by bankruptcy—when it was all really caused by the top managers, who, because of personal problems or disagreement over how to run the company, did not cooperate with each other.

In such situations, the real, true, and direct cause of the trouble is masked by the effects of that cause. Since most people are very reluctant to openly discuss their failures, especially if the reasons are personal, you are very unlikely to ever hear about the real and direct cause of corporate failure. I don't mind discussing the deep and difficult problems we had within our own small business because of the mistakes I made in selecting my corporate associates, because we overcame those problems. We survived and grew. But if the problems had caused the failure of our new venture (and it came very close to doing just that), I wouldn't write about it. Even if I did write on the subject, you wouldn't want to read about some guy who is whining about his business failure and blaming it all on others.

I will end this chapter with an opinion that I am unable to substantiate with statistics. I believe that the selection of partners and business associates is one of the main reasons for eventual success or failure in any small business. Only the effects of good or bad personal business relationships among the principal owners show on the books and records for later examination, analysis, and review. In choosing your partners you determine the eventual success or failure of your new venture. You can learn from many of the mistakes you will make and can repair some situations. An error in this area is very difficult and sometimes impossible to rectify, so you have to do this well the first time—or else.

Other entrepreneurs with whom I have discussed this situation agree that this is one of the most important determinants of later success or failure. I have never met anyone who felt that the choice of close associates as business partners was an unimportant factor in the success or failure of a new business venture.

4

Motivating Others

As the entrepreneur of a small new business venture, you will have the important and continuing responsibility of motivating others, but you should require very little external motivation for yourself. Any leader who requires periodic motivation to maintain his interest or to keep sharp has a serious problem. Who will motivate you? You must be self-motivating. I don't mean that you are not allowed to ever get depressed or seek a word of compassion and understanding. Many great leaders have found it beneficial to have people in whom they can confide or with whom they can discuss problems, and thereby let off steam now and then.

In the small business, you can't afford to hire and pay for a confidant. In addition, it is dangerous for a leader to discuss doubts and concerns with subordinates, who may be shaken by disclosures of delicate information. Like it or not, the lead person in any organization becomes a parent figure. The leader can't reveal his own fears, concerns, doubts, or lack of knowledge to very many people. In fact, it upsets many employees to hear the boss say "I don't know," or "I feel down today," or "I'm depressed." This is espe-cially true in the small business, where the leader is highly visible and accessible.

The entrepreneur must be a self-motivator who handles his own periods of depression or uncertainty at work. The entrepreneur is the coach—he gives the pep talks and motivates the team. Whoever heard of a coach needing or receiving a motivational lec-ture? If you need constant reassurance and you look to others for approving smiles and general agreement, your small business is in for trouble.

To lead properly, you must be able to take responsibility for making decisions and for deciding on courses of action. If you're successful you will be called lucky, and if you fail you will be called dumb. If that bothers you, then pack it all in while you can. The job will eventually wear you down. (I used to get upset when, after days and weeks of hard, sustained effort that led to a new contract and growth, people would call me "lucky." Now, I just smile and tell them I am going to get lucky again two weeks from next Wednesday.)

As you progress higher up the corporate ladder, you receive less personal supervision and direction and your responsibility be-comes broader. You will have more things to do, but you will have the freedom to choose how to spend your time; you'll decide what things to do when. No one likes distasteful or unpleasant duties, such as disciplining or dismissing subordinates or facing high- or low-level disagreements. However, those things must be done. Some leaders avoid such issues by delaying, obfuscating, or, worse, assigning the task to a subordinate. (One of my former managers would send me to meetings at which he expected trouble, so that I would take the heat. Eventually, clients would bypass him and call me directly. Later, I was invited to visit a client's facility that was out of state. They specified in their telegram that my boss was not to attend. Avoiding unpleasant duties cost him plenty in the way of further advancement.)

Here's how I force myself to do what has to be done. First I set a date by which I will attempt to solve the problem once and for all. Next I tell my secretary, my assistant, and several senior managers of my plan. Now I am committed. I have jumped into the water and I have to swim. I can't turn back or avoid the issue—if I do, everyone who knows about the problem will conclude that I lack the moral fiber to deal with an unpleasant situation. I recommend that you set up a similarly self-motivating procedure, in which you have little choice except to do what you have promised when you said you would. It has certainly worked well for me over the years.

Now let's discuss how the leader motivates the team. It is obvious to most of us that different people will respond to different stimuli so we have to find out what motivates most people. However, be aware that what motivates you, as the entrepreneur, will very likely not motivate your employees, at least not with the same intensity.

A few years ago I read the results of a study conducted by the U.S. Chamber of Commerce that compared what motivates managers with what motivates non-managers.* People in each group were given a list of ten reasons for working and told to arrange the items in order of importance. The difference between the two groups was startling. The highly paid management group listed salary first, opportunity for promotion (more salary) second, and job security (keeping the salary) third. The lower paid workers, however, listed a meaningful job first, kind and understanding supervisor second, pleasant co-workers third, and good working conditions fourth. The second group listed money fifth in importance and opportunity for promotions or job security even lower on the list.

The people who were earning high salaries worked for and wanted even more money. The lower paid workers weren't too interested in earning higher salaries. This may well be the reason that

---

*"What Do Employees Want?" *Cars & Trucks Magazine*, February 1970, p. 47.

the lower paid group remains that way—by their own admission, these people don't consider salary to be very important, as long as they are doing a job they like, in an environment they like, and with people they like. Their goals at work seem to be more social than personal.

How can this information be of value to you as an entrepreneur? If you are highly motivated by money, do not assume that your staff is too. If you try to motivate your staff with money, you may be surprised to find that there is no enthusiastic response. In fact, you may not see any reaction at all, or you may see an adverse response.

As an example, consider my experience with an employee. I had a contract falling behind schedule and called on a senior analyst to move into the new area to support the site manager as necessary. I established a deadline and told him that if he finished the task before then, I would award him a $2,000 bonus. He immediately showed anger and concern and told me that I didn't have to bribe him to do his job. He resented my approach and felt that I was questioning his ability and integrity. I replied that I was trying to stimulate and reward him, not bribe him. In any case, he finished the job on time and refused to accept the bonus.

His response so stupefied me that, later on, I asked him to explain why he got so upset when I offered him a bonus. He replied that the offer of a bonus over and above his normal pay indicated that I believed he was not giving his best effort and therefore had to offer him more money to get him to do his best.

I also discovered that there was little if any acknowledgment or response from most employees when I paid cash Christmas bonuses. Most people considered it the same as their salary. I had transferred my primary motivation for work (earning money) to the staff and they did not have the same set of priorities that I had, so I didn't get a good response. In discussing this situation with other small business entrepreneurs, we found similar reactions to cash awards. A friend of mine who owns a new-car dealership gave me the solution. The car manufacturers give not only cash awards for meeting or exceeding sales quotas, but also presents, vacation trips, special banquets, trophies, and letters of achievement—and they get a tremendous response.

The following Christmas I bought every employee a digital wristwatch. The response was overwhelming. I received thank-you notes from everyone. In following years I gave employees TV sets, tape recorders, portable AM/FM radios, cameras, and so on. Every year the response was excellent. We started to receive thank-you notes from the spouses and even the children of some employees, because they used the presents at home and were most appreciative. Since the idea of bonuses is to reward and motivate the employees, I was finally on the right track.

Frankly, though, I'll never understand why I get a thank-you note from an employee who has received a portable TV set worth $150 but get no response when that same person receives a bonus check large enough to purchase 10 TV sets. I suppose that paid vacations for two to places like Bermuda, the Bahamas, Paris, or London elicit a tremendous response because few of us ever get to go to such places. And employees probably wouldn't spend bonus money on such a luxury. I strongly recommend that you consider offering gifts, paid vacations, dinner parties, and so on to motivate employees, instead of cash bonuses. Perhaps a combination of the two may be useful.

Remember, try to give the employees what they want and what motivates them, not what you think they should want. If you have ever tried to convince your child to major in a "useful" subject in college, such as engineering, math, science, or business, when your child wants to study medieval theater and ballads, you know how fruitless it is to impose your judgment or choices on others. It's the same with the employees; they want what they want. They respond to what motivates them, and no lecture from you or anyone else will change that. Accept it and act accordingly, and both you and your staff will be motivated, responsive, and contented.

Sometimes a personal letter of appreciation for a job well done accompanied by a personalized pen and pencil set engraved with the company logo can be an effective motivator, especially if only a few people have them. It's a good idea to periodically vary the small item; tie clips, pens and pencils, bracelets, desk sets, and fancy desk name plates are all well received. For higher level personnel, new office furniture, rugs, corner offices with a view, reserved parking spaces, and other such perks are, in many situations, very well received.

A friend of mine was in charge of his company's move from an old office building to a new one. He told me that each senior executive was allowed to spend up to $10,000 to decorate his own office in the new building. The executives were delighted and each one spent a great deal of time choosing the right desk, table lamp, rug, or whatever. So even senior managers who are motivated by money will respond to non-monetary presents and benefits.

You might also consider creating a special award to increase productivity and raise employee morale. At one place I worked, each month an employee was selected as "Employee of the Month," with the following rewards:

1. The employee's picture was taken with the general manager and the picture appeared on the front page of the company newsletter.
2. The winner received a special badge to wear at work for one month.
3. The winner could park his car in the front of the building, in a specially marked parking space (next to the general manager's car) for one month.
4. The winner could enter the building for one month via the front door, which was usually reserved for executives and visitors.

I expected that the people in my department would think the award was as childish as I thought it was. But when I observed the winners proudly wearing their special badges and parking out front—even though that meant a much longer walk through the building to where they worked—I had to reconsider my skepticism. The award really worked. People were motivated and production did go up.

Now let's consider how to motivate the first-time manager who has been promoted from within the company. If he does not fully accept the responsibilities of the new role and continues to perform the duties of his old job, his other management and administrative responsibilities will go unattended or will be assigned to a subordinate.

It's up to you to very clearly and precisely define, preferably in writing and in advance, what you consider the new manager's areas of responsibility to be. Go over it, in detail, with the manager-to-be, and get his approval and acceptance of the new responsibilities before he takes over. Closely (on a weekly or even daily basis) monitor the situation for a month or two. If the new manager settles in, fine—you have no problem. But sometimes a new manager doesn't fully accept in his own mind all of the new responsibilities pertinent to his new role. In that case, you have a problem.

Small businesses seem to be in a constant state of flux, and it is very easy to assign new people to new jobs without taking the time for a formal job review like the one described above. But it takes so little time to conduct a formal job review in advance and it saves so much time later that it is well worth the effort. I have seen some people refuse to accept a promotion after being thoroughly apprised of their new responsibilities. That's preferable to failing later because they were unaware of what they were getting into.

Even in large well-established companies, new managers are sometimes left to their own devices and, in many cases, serious problems follow.

Ideally, every manager should be self-motivating. You can't *instill* initiative in anyone, but you can direct and channel existing initiative into the proper or desired course. In order to do that, you must maintain close and open communication. In a marriage, a very serious problem arises when the couple stops communicating with each other. When this occurs and becomes the routine course of behavior, the end of the marriage is generally near. The same is true between superiors and subordinates up and down the chain of command. At our company, we require that each level of management sees or speaks to the levels above and below it at least once a day. If you have an open working relationship and people are well motivated, then you will have plenty to talk about. In this way, with each level communicating with the one above and the one below each and every day, problems or difficulties are brought to the attention of people at the proper level on the same day they develop.

Employee morale matters very much and it's up to you to set the tone for the entire operation. Junior managers will usually imitate you for one of two reasons. They may admire and respect you so much that they act toward their subordinates in the same way as you act toward them. Or they may be trying to "make points" with you by showing you how they follow orders. In either case, the morale of the entire operation stems from the top person.

In addition to the various methods and techniques described earlier in this chapter for stimulating, motivating, and maintaining morale in employees, a free, open, and honest channel of communication right to the top is probably the single most important motivating factor. People like to feel that their opinions matter and will be heard, even if their suggestions are not always followed or their requests are dented. If they receive no response or are ridiculed or dressed down for trying to be heard, morale will be negatively affected. As long as each person goes through proper channels, he or she will be heard and will receive a response quickly. In our company, there are no secrets or replies via the grapevine—there's just a plain, open, and direct response. Win or lose, most people value this policy above all others.

5 ──────────────────────────────

How and When to Start

There are three basic forms your new enterprise can take: (1) a proprietorship, (2) a partnership, or (3) a corporation. Neither one is better than the other two; they are just different from one another. The type most appropriate to your enterprise depends on what you want to do, why, and how big you plan to become. Each has its own specific advantages and disadvantages, and it is important for you to carefully think out, before you start, the type of business you want and the goals you want to achieve. The proprietorship is the simplest. There are no elaborate, expensive, or complicated forms to fill out and very few legal procedures to observe at first. Taxes are lowest in this case, in comparison with the corporation, but a proprietorship is not entitled to many tax deductions available to partnerships or corporations. You can get going without a lawyer, CPA, or anyone else. It's easy, but that can cause future problems.

You may be a working person who cannot afford the initial expenses of adequate legal and CPA services at the start. You may know all about your own work, whether it's TV repairs, carpentry, retail sales, or landscape gardening, but as your new enterprise prospers and grows and you hire more people to work for you, you will get into serious trouble if you are not knowledgeable about the financial or legal aspect of the business. Social Security, workers' compensation, minimum wage laws, insurance, fringe benefits, employees' rights, safety regulations, tax forms, payroll deductions, and a plethora of other state and federal regulations, far too numerous to list here, will come into play. If you overlook just one, it can stop you dead in your tracks. Ignorance is no excuse.

The ease and simplicity of starting a proprietorship will eventually catch up with you unless you plan thoroughly in advance and choose the form of your business for good and sufficient reasons, not because you are unaware of any of the alternatives.

I know a man who had a small grocery store in the 1930s. He was unable to refuse giving groceries out, on credit, to people who would send their children in with a note for bread, milk, and meat for supper. He knew they wouldn't eat if he refused. He went bankrupt. He then opened a restaurant and many times the cooks, waiters, and waitresses would go home with more money than he would. He failed again. However, he eventually ended up as president of a bank on Cape Cod, where he was able to follow good business sense in making decisions. He said he could handle a corporation but he was not very good as a proprietor. He was able to refuse credit to corporations, but not to individuals on a personal, face-to-face basis. At the bank he used his business judgment; as a proprietor, he used his feelings and emotions.

In a proprietorship, your personal and company finances are one and the same; if you owe a business debt, it can be collected from your personal assets—your house, personal bank account, or car. If a proprietor has little or no business experience, he can inadvertently get business and company assets and debts so mixed up and confused that no one can straighten them out. This can be a great hazard, so think about it carefully.

The partnership is very similar to the proprietorship, but with other potential problems that you should carefully consider in advance. In partnerships, you have to satisfy your partners as well as the customers. Internal bickering and arguments over who does what, why, when, and how can result, and there will probably be differences of opinion on how to run the business. At the start of a business, very few things are ever in order and sudden and unexpected events require prompt and decisive action. In a partnership, the leader may not be able to act quickly and do what he thinks best; the partners will want to have a say in those actions that will affect their interests. This results in leadership by committee, which involves discussion and persuasion rather than prompt direction. That can be deadly in the young enterprise.

It is not unusual for partners to disagree regularly and then to actually stop talking to one another. How does one run a business when the principals aren't even speaking to one another? I'm sure I don't know, yet people try it. Some do succeed, but the failure rate far exceeds the success rate in those cases.

Another risk of a partnership is the possibility that each partner can be held personally liable for all of the debts of the venture. Even if you have only a 10 percent interest in the partnership, you can later be held personally liable for 100 percent of the debts. Guard against this very carefully, especially if the partnership becomes very successful—you do not want to be held liable if any big problem ever arises later on. If the partnership makes a $200,000 annual profit and you are a 10 percent partner, you earn $20,000 per year. However, suppose the partnership loses $200,000, which it can't afford to pay, and that the partners who hold the other 90 percent pay only $50,000 from their personal assets. Now suppose that your home, bank account, cars, and so on have a value in excess of $150,000. In that case, you will be required to pay $150,000—75 percent of the debt of the partnership. This may not seem fair, but it happens, so be very careful about whom you choose in a partnership arrangement. Be sure to obtain competent legal advice. Have everything explained to you very carefully *before* you embark on a partnership.

With respect to the corporation, there's an old legal saying: "Perhaps only God can make a tree, but only a lawyer can make a corporation." You can't incorporate on your own, unless you really know what you are doing, so don't try. Get the services of a very good corporate attorney or, better still, a law firm that specializes in this sort of business. Your family lawyer may not be the best person in this case. Get some advise from banks about lawyers, and then investigate several possibilities. This is a very important step. It takes a competent lawyer to set up a corporation; if you use someone who does it poorly, you won't find out about the lawyer's incompetence until it's too late.

The advantages of the corporation over the proprietorship and partnership lie mainly in the area of corporate liability. As head of a corporation, you risk only your primary investment in the company. The corporation is a separate legal entity and as such shields you from further personal financial loss should the company later lose money or go into bankruptcy. To return to the case of a $200,000 debt that the company can't pay, you *personally* are liable for none of it unless it can be proved in court that you participated in an illegal maneuver to protect your own personal interest. If you expect your venture to grow to a considerable size, the corporation may be the form for you to use right from the start.

The main disadvantage of the corporate structure is the amount of taxes you must pay before you receive your dividends. One dollar in pretax corporate profit can be subject to federal corporation taxes of approximately 50 percent, followed by (in some states) an additional 8 or 10 percent state tax. This reduces the dollar to 40¢. If your personal income is sufficiently high, then you can pay up to 70 percent additional personal taxes to the federal government on the 40¢ dividend you received, again followed by another 8 to 10 percent state income tax, depending upon where you reside. This reduces your original pretax dollar to less than 10¢ for you to spend, as the stockholder. If you save or reinvest that dime, it's taxed all over again. You may ask, "What's the point of even trying, if I lose 90¢ out of every dollar in pretax profit?" That's a good question and there's a good answer.

Generally, the new corporation does not pay dividends at first. It retains the income for future growth, and few if any dividends are paid during the first several years. As the company grows, its stock becomes more and more valuable, and the way it makes a big gain is in the later sale of stock to willing buyers, for a share in a growing, prosperous, and successful new venture. Now it is subject to capital gains taxes, if the stock is held for a sufficient period of time. Fortunately, capital gains taxes are well below taxes paid from profit, which are then taxed again as unearned income (dividends to the owners). If your venture prospers, you can see why competent legal advice and guidance is mandatory if you opt for the corporate structure when you start your venture. And if you start out as a proprietorship or partnership, and your venture grows, it's very likely that you will change over to the corporate structure—so give that alternative some thought in advance.

Subchapter S of the Internal Revenue Code allows you to form a legal corporation and still treat corporate income as personal income, thereby avoiding corporate income taxes on profits. There are special rules and regulations concerning the number of stockholders and so on that you should be aware of. A Subchapter S corporation combines the advantages of all three forms of business into one, but you'll need a lawyer to figure it all out and explain it to you. As your corporation grows, it can then be changed over to a regular corporation at the appropriate time.

Whether to choose a proprietorship, partnership, or corporation as the form of your business venture is very important as time goes on. Neither I nor anyone can tell you which is best for your operation—that depends on what your ultimate plans are for your business. Generally, a proprietorship or partnership won't survive the departure of the principals. The corporation is immortal and can outlast any and all of the founders, whose families and estates can continue to earn from their shares of stock.

If you invite other people to join you in your venture, do not assume that offering them a share in the enterprise will automatically get and hold their attention and loyalty. Although they will stand to gain a great deal by the increase in value of their shares as the company prospers and grows, their reaction may not be what you expect. This situation is discussed in detail in Chapter 3, but I mention it here for emphasis.

You must also consider how to handle your company money. There are two basic accounting options open to you: cash and accrual. In the cash system, you record and report only actual cash paid and received. In the accrual method, you account for the cash flow over the period of time in which it was earned or spent rather than when it was paid or received. For example, suppose you paid a $12,000 insurance premium in January for the coming year. In the cash system you would record the whole $12,000 as an outlay for January, and none for the rest of the year. In the accrual system, you would list it as a $1,000 expense each month during the year, because it is really spent at the rate of $1,000 per month. If you worked on a project for three months at $5,000 per month, and you were paid during the fourth month, the cash system would list no income for three months, and $15,000 as cash income in the fourth month. The accrual system would list $5,000 earned for each of the three months during which you actually did the job.

The accrual system seems like the most businesslike accounting method, because the books more truly reflect how your company actually earned money or incurred expenses. Anyone looking over the books of an accounting system based on the accrual method could very easily see how the company operates and when and how the funds are earned and spent.

However, there are many types of businesses in which the cash system may be advantageous. Small operations of a few people may not require the elaborate and expensive bookkeeping system necessary for the accrual method. Certain seasonal types of operations or businesses, in which income fluctuates, may opt for the cash system. In choosing your accounting system, it's best to follow the advice of a good CPA. An inexperienced or untrained person who attempts to keep his own books is practicing false economy.

An example taken from my own experience illustrates one of the problems with the accrual accounting system. As the end of one fiscal year approached, we were owed over $200,000, which we had logged in according to the accrual system. Most of the money was owed to us by the federal government, which can be maddeningly erratic in its payment schedules. We had to make out, file, and pay our corporate income tax, and we owed Uncle Sam $20,000 at the same time that Uncle Sam owed us $180,000. I asked our lawyer and our accountant if we could explain our situation, file the tax form, and tell the IRS to get the $20,000 that we owed them from the government agency that owed us $180,000. The reply I got was, "Sure you can, Bill—if you want to go to jail." So we borrowed $20,000 and paid up, and also paid interest on the loan.

As you can see, the accrual system carries accounts receivable as an asset. This means that money owed to the corporation is "assumed" to be eventually collectible, and sometimes it is not. Also, the accrual system can carry on the books a large inventory of goods as an asset. What if you can't sell the inventory?

If you use the accrual system you should understand accounting methods and terminology. Take a one-semester course at a local school; it will be well worth your time. Then when accountants compute your current ratio or acid-test ratio on your balance sheet, you will know they are simply trying to find out how much cash you have on hand. Since the perennial problem of most small business ventures is the cash-flow problem, you may be treated by lenders as if you are on the cash system whether you are or not. Therefore, you should understand both accounting methods and choose the one that you think is best for you. By law, you are permitted to change over at the start of any business or fiscal year, but if you do the tax people will look carefully at your operation. They will want to make sure that you aren't changing over to achieve some short-term gain or to avoid payment of taxes that may fall due under one system but not under the other. Once again, competent CPA and legal advice is required in this situation.

Some unpleasant words are necessary here concerning the lawyers and CPAs you choose. The majority are hard-working and honest people who will do their best for you. However, there are some who will consider their own interests over and above you, your business, or anything else. It's best to have them give you their advice and recommendations in writing before you act. You hired them to give you expert legal and accounting advice and services, and if they are reluctant to advise you in writing, and if they avoid giving you specific opinions and options available to you with their written recommendations, then be careful. They may not be certain how to react and may not want a written record of their involvement in your decisions. They can be held liable for grossly inferior performance, but it's up to you to prove it, so it's best to have it all written down. I'm not saying you shouldn't put any faith and trust in your legal and accounting advisers, but I am saying to be careful. If they are wrong, you lose and they don't, so act accordingly.

A close friend of mine had a lawyer on his board of directors who had been with the company as corporate secretary since its inception. In the early years, the founders could not afford to put much money into the business. The company was growing nicely but was undercapitalized. As the company grew, its need for working capital increased, and management was forced to take out short-term loans to meet the monthly payroll. At a board meeting, the lawyer offered to buy a 25 percent interest in the company for $100,000, to help provide working capital. Just a few months previously, the company had turned down an offer of $2.4 million for a 100 percent interest. My friend reminded the lawyer (who had handled the unsuccessful merger negotiations) of the $2.4-million offer, and asked what he thought the company was worth. The lawyer withdrew his offer. Clearly, the lawyer was not representing his client, the corporation, at all; he was trying to get a good deal for himself.

You must choose professional services carefully. In general, older, established law and accounting firms tend to be less likely to try such shenanigans; they have their reputation to consider. They will probably be more expensive, but you get what you pay for. Also, larger firms have more business contacts and they may help you get new business via other clients, whom they know about.

How can you get start-up capital?

1. By putting it up yourself.
2. By selling shares in your new venture.
3. By borrowing from people or banks.
4. By using venture capital companies.

If you are able to draw on your own resources for all the money you need, then you have no problem and you needn't read further. Otherwise, you'll have to sell shares in your new venture or borrow the money.

If you sell shares, you will have to give up a portion of your ownership, and you won't get very much for each share at the start. People are wary about investing in new ventures, since many fail and the stockholder can end up with nothing.

If you borrow money, even as a corporation, the lenders will most likely want a pledge of your personal assets to back up what is, to them, an unsecured loan. If your corporation net worth doesn't exceed the loan you want at the start, no bank or lending institution that I know of will grant you a loan without your personal assets as collateral.

There are companies that specialize in lending venture capital to new entrepreneurs. I have had no personal experience with such firms, but you should consider them as a potential source of start-up or support funds for your new venture.

Be sure to consult with your lawyer and certified public account-ant about any large lending institution. Go to as many as you can and compare one against the other before you decide. I know from personal experience that arrangements with banks vary widely. We were seeking an open line of credit for $100,000 and wanted to pledge our corporate assets as security. The bank we chose gave us just that. However, one bank wanted us to leave a "compensat-ing balance" of an average of $15,000 in our corporate checking account. Another bank wanted our corporate officers to sign over their homes as security.

So shop around for your loan and study each proposal care-fully. Be aware that you can "haggle" or negotiate with banks. In fact, use the same techniques that you use when buying a car or a house: *Never* accept the first offer. In most cases, you can negotiate a better deal. You are buying and paying for the use of the money in the same way as you buy a car. Don't every say, "The bank gave me a loan." Bankers don't *give* you anything, they *sell* it to you. Also, don't thank them, let them thank you, because you are the client. The car dealer thanks you, right? Let the bank managers thank you for doing business with their bank.

We have discussed what form your venture can take, what ac-counting systems there are, and how to get the funds you need. It's not easy to put it all together, but no one ever said it is easy to start up a new venture. Just know what you are getting into before you start. Good strategy and good tactics are necessary for success of any venture, and both require careful advance thought and planning.

Running out of funds is not the cause of a small business's problems, it is the effect of other problems. If you don't carefully plan your funding arrangements, your venture won't make it. You may have to borrow money intially, but in the long run you can't finance your operation by any source other than good solid profit. Even New York City was pulled up short when it tried to borrow from one source to pay another. There's no free lunch.

In addition to the what, the why, and the how, timing is very important. There are good and bad times in our economy and economists have studied and written and argued about the economic business cycle ad nauseam in order to predict the swings in the economy, which nevertheless can be unpredictable.

Almost every good business school in the country produces a complex computer-oriented model of the econometrics of the business cycle. These models are good at explaining what happened in the past, but none has proved to be an accurate predictor of future business activity. If anyone ever develops a model that can be used to predict the business cycle, he would be foolish to publicize it. He should use the model to help him become rich in a very short time.

Smart people who have made it big had to take risks to get where they are. Once they're successful, someone else goes backward to figure out how it happened. The future is never predictable; we just plan what we want to do, try our darndest, and hope for the best.

When asked how he became so wealthy and successful, Bernard Baruch is reported to have replied, "It's easy: Buy when everyone is selling, and sell when everyone is buying." In other words, go against the trend. But that's easier said than done. That's what our government continually tries to do. It works to improve business activity during an economic downturn, and when things pick up, it tries to combat inflation by working to slow the growth of business. Unfortunately, the government doesn't seem to have been too successful at achieving its goals.

Nevertheless, timing in what you want to do is very important. In general, it is not a good idea to start a new venture during a recession—but certain businesses might be able to prosper. Consider that the following things go up during a recession:

1. The sale of home improvement tools, paint, rakes, shovels, and so on.
2. The incidence of divorce.
3. The incidence of heart attacks.

During a recession, more people are laid off, and they may do chores around the house that they had no time for when they were working. Since they will be buying the necessary equipment and supplies, it may not be a bad time to open a hardware or paint supply store. Marital problems seem to erupt when husbands and wives are home all day together. (When Mrs. Hubert Humphrey was asked how she liked having her husband home all day long, after he was not elected to the Presidency, she replied: "I married him for better or worse, but not for lunch.") A recession may be a good time to enter the field of marriage counseling.

If you plan to operate a seasonal business, be prepared for the uneven timing of cash income and outflow. Your fiscal year should not end at high or low periods in your cycle. For example, if you run a gift shop and sell Christmas cards and calendars, you should figure out well in advance how to handle the rush from September to December and how to handle the lull for the rest of the year. Perhaps you should try to sell products or services that are in season when your major stock items are not, such as bathing suits and other summer items. If you were to add winter sports items to your gift shop, you would only intensify the cyclical nature of your business. You would have to hire a large temporary staff for several months a year and lay off most of your workers during the summer months. You can't get and retain a good staff that way—and you wouldn't deserve one.

Timing is also important in technological or scientific areas, where someone else's technological breakthrough can put you under very quickly. In the computer industry, many good companies, small and large, have failed because their product or service was introduced at the wrong time.

Don't overlook timing—it can make or break your new venture. Bigger companies can ride out an economic downturn of one to three years, but few small ventures can survive such a downturn. Some economic theorists (who probably have never had to meet a payroll) state that this situation is good for the economy: The businesses that survive a downturn are the "fittest." With fewer companies left and with competition reduced, the survivors are lean and ready to bound into the marketplace. They are more reasonable in price, more responsive to the customers, and more prepared for rapid growth. Sounds sort of like a jungle, doesn't it? In some ways, it is. Although "Economic Darwinism" may be for the best in the long run, that is little solace to the lambs who are killed off in the process.

It behooves you, then, to grow as rapidly as you can. If you can't become a corporate tiger, at least grow sharp teeth so you can grab hold of your share of the market and can protect against the tigers that will threaten your area of interest.

6

Typical Early Problems

A corporation has a life of its own that is separate, distinct, and independent from its founders and owners. The corporation can be immortal. A business acquaintance was working in London several years ago. He was forced to move from his apartment because the lease on the land on which the apartment building stood had expired. Everyone had to vacate the building so it could be torn down and replaced by a high-rise office building. That wouldn't be very unusual, except for the fact that the lease that had expired was 900 years old.

The corporate body and the human body have many similarities. Like the human infant, the corporate infant is very vulnerable during the first year or two of its life. Infant mortality rates, which are carefully computed by insurance companies, are very high. Corporate babies, too, have a mortality rate that is very much higher than the adult corporate rate. The failure rate for new businesses is higher than 50 percent for the first year and is between 60 and 70 percent for the first two years of corporate life.

When humans become teenagers, they must cope with certain emotional, physical, and psychological problems. A teenager has an adult's body, but the mind and emotions of a child. This, of course, is a very trying time for both adolescents and their parents. If a company survives to become a corporate teenager, it too undergoes growing pains and experiences psychological problems. The small business atittudes, procedures, and techniques that helped it survive and grow may no longer apply. The company must change or die—it can't remain static. Some companies go under in their teen years because they can't and won't adjust to what they have become. They look backward instead of forward. As Churchill said, "They have their feet firmly planted in mid-air, resolutely facing the rear."

Corporations become old, just as people do. Corporate arthritis, circulatory problems, and even senility set in with few realizing it. Old management becomes set in its ways, out of date, and resistant to change, and thus becomes inefficient. The corporate arteries become clogged and the old company quietly slows down and passes away.

The major problems occur at the beginning; teenage and old-age problems can be dealt with if you prepare for them in advance. The managers of a successful and growing small enterprise usually have the time and resources to work on problems, but they avoid change fanatically. In such cases, it is difficult or even impossible to solve problems.

At the start, however, the errors in management result mainly from ignorance exhibited by the founding entrepreneurs. As one SBA adviser told me, "Many technical entrepreneurs have advanced degrees, and they are very intelligent and well trained in their line of work. The reason they fail in business is not because they don't know the answers. It is because they don't know the questions." *Amen!*

Let's discuss some typical early problems that can cause the small venture great difficulty. The first problem is failure to prepare written goals and to make specific plans for achieving them. This subject was discussed in Chapter 2. Running out of money was discussed in Chapter 5. As mentioned, the cash-flow problem is an effect of other problems. In racing around and trying to borrow money to stem the negative cash-flow problem, the entrepreneur may be trying to solve the wrong problem. In fact, a far more serious problem probably requires his attention. He may be rushing around to banks trying to borrow capital, when his real problem is excessive production costs or poor pricing strategies or a low level of sales. A cash loan to someone in this situation only postpones the inevitable. His corporate body is bleeding and he's trying to get a transfusion with his wounds still unattended. In such cases, the cash flows in one place and out another.

Internal Bickering

This has destroyed many good small ventures early on. It is a strange quirk of human nature that there is often little trouble or few arguments when things are going badly—everyone works long and hard to make the small venture survive and grow. However, as conditions improve and growth occurs people suddenly start to argue over minor and pointless things. Egos start to come into play. As people begin to believe that the new venture is well on its way, some turn their thoughts, activities, and efforts away from the prime goal, which is survival and growth of the company. Their new activities and behavior may impede the company's growth and profits. Now there's some money to spend. Fine, who gets it? The president wants to retain all earnings for use within the company, to contribute to future growth or to reduce borrowing for working capital. Other principals want dividends. They want to increase their standard of living right now, so it will reflect their newly acquired status as officers of a growing and prosperous company. "Let's buy several new company cars to impress people. What about the office? Shouldn't we move now to more lavish and larger quarters?

How about new and expensive office furniture to impress everyone? That is sure to get us more business." Is it really? Many think so, but I don't.

There is nothing wrong with living up to a standard that you can afford. However, when people, companies, or even governments start to live beyond their means, they are borrowing against the future (remember New York City?). Sooner or later you have to pay the piper. Although this sort of thing can go on for some time before it catches up with large corporations or well-insulated governments, it won't take long to catch up with the small business venture. And small entrepreneurs won't be able to get the government to rush in and help financially, because their presence or absence from the marketplace doesn't matter that much to the economy in general.

Personal Entanglements with Employees

In the close-knit informality of the new business venture, a camaraderie often develops and it is all too easy to become involved in the personal and family troubles of your employees. At first, you may be flattered that they seek your advice on a wide variety of personal problems, but if you encourage them you will find that you are spending an hour or two each day on such discussions. On some days, a line formed outside my office that reminded me of the line outside a confession box in church. However, I did not feel qualified to give the advice I was being asked for, since I am not a psychologist, marriage counselor, or financial expert. Some people had serious home and personal problems, and kept coming back over and over again. Before I knew what was happening, I was in over my head. When I tried to withdraw, I created some resentment, because some people felt I should keep on helping and advising them.

People didn't stop coming completely until I advised everyone that my door is always open, but only to people with job-related problems. I suggested that those who needed advice on personal matters turn to professionals, such as priests, ministers, rabbis, doctors, or counselors, or to close relatives or friends. As the entrepreneur or lead person, you will be regarded by your employees as a father figure and will be approached with very personal and intimate problems. If you feel you are able to handle personal situations and feel you are qualified to give important advice, then use your own judgment and proceed with caution. I just wasn't qualified to advise a woman on whether she should forgive or leave her husband, or tell a parent how to handle a child on drugs. It all overwhelmed me, and I backed out rapidly.

I mention this as a typical early problem because other small business managers have confirmed its occurrence and persistence. They all got involved, as I did, and they all had to pull out. It was taking too much of their time and they saw they were not qualified to offer opinions in such serious personal situations.

Rigidity

As you start to grow, opportunities will arise from unforeseen or unanticipated places, just as problems will. As a result, you will have to be able to quickly switch direction to seize a fleeting opportunity. If any of your principals or senior people are too rigid to react to the changing environment, or they do not want to change jobs for the good of the company, you have a problem.

Decentralization

As you grow in size and begin to differentiate functions, you may set up several separate divisions under your direction. For many companies, the next step is to make those divisions independent cost centers, which can be advantageous for accounting purposes. However, be careful that the managers of each cost center don't become so concerned with their group that they work at cross purposes to overall company interest. Let me present some examples:

As we grew, we developed several good major accounts. We set up separate departments to handle each account. After a short while, I noticed that each department manager was losing interest in the affairs of other departments. At a meeting to discuss general, overall company goals—profit, expansion, and so on—I noticed that each manager was concerned only with his own department's affairs. When I wanted to transfer people from Group A to Group B, I immediately got a negative reaction from Group A's manager, who said he was "losing good people." In spite of my repeated statements that we have only one interest, and that is company growth and profit, the message didn't sink in. Internal company competition and bickering caused us serious problems at the highest level. It persists even to this day. That old willing cooperation to do anything for the company started to erode. Each manager wanted to look better, on paper, than the others. In an attempt to remedy this problem, we have made management bonuses contingent on overall corporate profit, so if one group does very well at the expense of the others, all share in the overall benefit.

But I haven't solved this problem yet, because I don't know how to motivate a manager to run his own operation to the best of his ability and produce maximum results, and yet support overall corporate goals to the extent of decreasing his own department's efficiency and profit. Perhaps the problem results from the fact that we are asking people to think at two different levels at the same time, or to wear two hats. This is difficult for anyone to do.

Of course, there comes a time when you must establish separate cost and reporting centers, but don't do it too early or you may never recover.

Competition from Within

In a growing company, your own staff may compete with you. Watch out for this. It can kill. A business acquaintance of mine started up a computer software programming company. He got a contract and then hired staff members, one by one, to augment his growing company. When he had about 9 employees, four of his senior staff members came to him at a crucial point in his contract and demanded a share in ownership in his new venture. They threatened to walk out, leaving him unable to complete his first sizable job, if he refused. This was blackmail, pure and simple. He said no, they walked out, and he went out of business.

Over a period of several years, my company lost seven key employees to our clients, who hired them because they were such excellent technical personnel. This was staggering to us, but we survived because it didn't happen all at once, as it did to my unfortunate business associate. Then I remembered that, as a condition of employment where I had formerly worked, I had signed a "no-conflict-of-interests agreement." I had our lawyer draw up a standard no-conflict-of-interests agreement for all our employees to sign. I was taken aback to find out that several senior people, including a corporate officer, did not want to sign it. We offered them a "sign-it-or-leave" ultimatum; two left and everyone else signed. We have never had a problem with this since.

I strongly recommend that you have your lawyer prepare such a standard agreement for all to sign, in advance, so you won't have to contend with competition from within. Competition is fine, but not from your own clients or staff. There's a big world out there. If any of our people want to try to make it, as we have, they have our blessings—but not with our clients or employees.

You will probably find that very few employees will object to signing a no-conflict-of-interests agreement at the start of their employment with you. At that point, they're not familiar with your clients or the way you operate. The agreement makes it clear to you, to them, and to everyone else that company interests come first. Most people I have met will honor such agreements. The problems come up when there are no agreements and people are free to pursue their own interests, in their own way.

Identifying the Market

Another perennial problem with new ventures is deciding how to sell your product, to whom, when, and at what price. Associated with this problem is your selection of clients. At first, the tendency is to find and grab any job you can. But think about this for a while Are you selling to the kind of client you want? Do you want 100 small clients, or four or five big ones? There's safety in numbers, of course, but many small jobs, the ones for less than $50,000, require a tremendous amount of accounting, pricing, and record keeping, and the number of delinquent accounts will be high. It has been my experience that it is easier to pursue and win a large contract than to manage many smaller and less profitable ones. If you pursue the small jobs, you are always vulnerable to competition from any firm that is just starting up. Small, shoestring operations can handle the three- to five-person jobs, and usually at a low price. If you concentrate your interests, efforts, and staff on these types of jobs, you will probably stay small, because you have to think, act, and price your product and service as a very small enterprise does. Your plan should include the pursuit of larger and larger tasks. You'll be surprised to find out what you are capable of. It's a question of judgment, of course, but it's best to try for larger projects, because that's the way any company grows. If you doubt your own ability to cope with such efforts, then perhaps it's time for a new top person to take over. The idea is for your small outfit to grow to medium size in order to out-compete small competitors.

In addition to knowing how to sell your product or service, it is equally important to know to whom to sell, when, and for how much. Let me repeat this, for emphasis: It has been our experience that larger jobs are easier to get, can be negotiated faster, and are simpler to execute than small jobs. In the small jobs, clients tend to want you to do too many extra things for which you receive no compensation (they can't afford it). One of our small contracts was with a state agency. The contract manager wanted us to attend a meeting with him every Friday to report on weekly progress. He called me several times each week to discuss the job, and, no matter how often I would refer him to our task manager, he kept trying to have several of us attend his weekly meetings. He focused that closely on the job because it was his only contract. With larger jobs, the customer's contract manager generally has other, more important responsibilities, and will turn the job over to you without meddling in day-to-day details. He judges your work by the final result. Having been involved in both small and large contracts, I strongly recommend the larger ones over the small ones.

Alfred Sloan, of General Motors, was a corporate success by any standard you wish to apply. Yet, in reviewing his life and work at GM, he wrote that at first he didn't think or act "big enough."* One can only wonder what GM might have become if Mr. Sloan had thought "big" right from the start.

Growing Too Fast

Now that we have discussed growing as rapidly as you can, let's discuss growing too big too soon. Once again, it's a question of judgment, but unfortunately growing too quickly can be as deadly as not growing at all. Grow according to your plan. If you find your growth is 30 percent greater than you had planned, it's time for a whole new plan.

Don't rush ahead blindly and accept all of the new business that you can get and hope for the best. Don't confuse growth with profit, for the complete opposite can be true. What if your profit margin is 10 percent and you borrow large sums at 14 or 15 percent to finance expansion? What if you borrow money to acquire new equipment and to hire a large staff to meet projected sales, and the orders don't materialize? What will you fall back on? No

*Alfred P. Sloan, Jr., *My Years with General Motors* (New York: Doubleday, 1964).

general ever enters a battle and deliberately cuts off his line of retreat, unless his situation is desperate and he has no other choice.

Sometimes, in the heady pursuit of new business, you can proceed too far, too fast. If an economic recession, an oil shortage, or a sudden increase in lending rates comes along, then "bang!" you are stopped short and with nowhere to go. If you are into the banks for loans and the loans fall due, you will be unable to refinance. Banks do not look kindly on any company asking to refinance a loan that is coming due, and it's difficult to borrow from Bank A to pay Bank B. In such cases, even if you get an extension or a second loan, the lending agency is very likely to demand that they have some sort of decision-making or veto power within your organization, to protect their interests. Do you want such interference? Whether you do or not is beside the point. You have to accept it, because "the money people" don't want to see you in bankruptcy courts. In such cases, no one wins—but you and your creditors lose the most.

Watch Your Step

To avoid the typical early problems, keep the following advice in mind:

Grow as fast as you can.	Don't grow too fast.
Help your personnel as much as you can.	Don't get involved in the personal lives of your employees.
Hire good people quickly.	Be careful whom you hire.
Be prepared to change your plan.	Grow via your plan.
Get all of the work you can.	Be selective in what you do.
Don't run out of money.	Be careful how you borrow.
Let your managers do their thing.	Watch out for internal bickering.

If the left-hand column of that list looks like the antithesis of the right-hand column, well, I suppose it is. The right-hand column is the conservative approach and the left-hand column the more liberal approach to management. You may be inclined to follow the advice in one column or to cross over and mix them up, but that's strictly up to you. There's no right or wrong way. It's your venture and it's up to you how you do it. (Nothing succeeds like success.) It's not easy, but no one said it was.

If you survive five or more years, you will be over the infant stage, and most of the corporate "teething problems" should then be well behind you.

7

Coping with
the Bureaucracy

As the entrepreneur of a small business venture, you will encounter the bureaucracy sooner or later. Whether you started your own venture because you were fed up with working in a bureaucracy or whether you've never come in contact with one, beware: you *will* encounter it, since most of the business you will want lies within a bureaucracy. Even though small businesses vastly outnumber the corporate giants, the top five or ten corporations in any field generally do 50 to 75 percent of all the business. The biggest bureaucracy of them all is the federal government, and that is a prime source of business for any small, medium-size, or large corporation. Therefore, you should know how to deal with bureaucrats.

I served in the Navy and worked as a civilian for the U.S. government for a combined period of almost nine years, and then worked for two corporate giants before I started my small business venture, so I have a pretty good idea of how bureaucracies operate. I did fairly well when I was within the bureaucracy and picked up techniques and methods that have helped me deal with it from the outside.

Large bureaucracies seem immortal: They just go on and on and on. It is to your advantage to do business with a large bureaucracy, because once you establish a working relationship it will endure. It may be difficult for you to get your first contract, but it is well worth the trouble.

As a small venture, you will have some tremendous advantages over a bureaucracy. You can change your own policies to adapt to changes in the relationship; a bureaucracy can't. Once you know the rules, you know how the bureaucrats will react, but they have no way of knowing how you or your company will respond. If you do change or modify a procedure the bureaucrats are familiar with, be sure to carefully explain how and why you changed whatever it is you changed. Bureaucrats don't change, and they tend to think that no one else does either.

We lost a sizable contract once, because I lowered our original bid during final negotiations and didn't explain why. The government personnel awarded the contract to a higher bidder because we hadn't explained and justified the price reduction. It never occurred to me that we could actually lose an award because we had lowered the price, but the bureaucracy had its procedures. I can understand why one has to justify a price increase, but not a decrease. What I didn't understand was that the bureaucracy requires justification for a price *change*. I learned the hard way.

Keep in mind that you can't beat the bureaucracy—it will win every time in a direct confrontation. You can, however, cope with it, if you are aware of how it operates. I have been deluged with forms and have provided the same information over and over again to various government agencies, which seem unable to communicate with one another. But I know I'm not alone and I also know that the bureaucracy won't change. It doesn't have to change, it will outlast and outlive us all, and it's pointless to attack it head on, even when you know you are right. It's bad enough to lose out when you are in the wrong or when the issue can be resolved either way, but it is very, very disturbing to have the bureaucracy beat you when you (and even the bureaucrats) know you are in the right.

If you go on a picnic and are harassed by a cow, dog, or even an elephant, you can deal with it. You can chase the cow away, give the dog a bone, or shoot the elephant, and then go on, undisturbed, with your picnic. However, what can you do if fog rolls in, or soldier ants attack your food? You have to retreat. The bureaucracy is, in many respects, like both the fog and the army of ants. You can see it and watch its activities, but nothing you do seems to have any effect on it. The bureaucracy has resources at its disposal that small organizations lack. There are times when the bureaucracy can respond with amazing speed and efficiency, but this happens only when some very high official from within the bureaucracy wants it to happen.

Uncooperative bureaucrats can, in the long run, defeat even those who are in charge of them. Consider the federal bureaucracy in Washington. It doesn't seem to matter very much who the President, Vice President, and top officials are, because the bureaucracy outlasts and outlives them all. Don't try to fight any bureaucracy. Even if you happen to win your argument, it will be a Pyrrhic victory, and you will be too exhausted or too damaged to fully exploit it.

Then how do you deal with it? The best way is to follow the old adage, "If you can't beat 'em, join 'em." If you deal with people who work in a bureaucracy in the same way that they deal with you, you might be very pleasantly surprised at the results. Let me present and discuss some examples.

1. One of the hallmarks of correspondence with the bureaucracy is that the person who writes you a letter usually tells you to reply to someone else, or to a code. If you follow those instructions, nothing will happen. As a rule, Mrs. X or Mr. Y or code PYJ-4-9-73-X won't know why you wrote, and won't call or write to you to find out. They are not working to make a profit, so they can outwait you. The best solution I have found to this situation is to write

directly back to your original contact. Always enclose a copy of the bureaucrat's letter as a reminder of what it's all about. Bureaucrats will tell you they have so much work to do that they can't be expected to remember everyone they've written to. No matter how many times an official tells you to write back to someone else, don't. Keep writing to the same person. If you keep writing directly to one bureaucrat and he wants you to stop, his best defense is to resolve the problem in question. If he tries to outlast you, be persistent. Let him know you won't stop writing until you are satisfied. You'll leave him no option but to resolve the problem at hand.

2. Suppose, after waiting for several months, you receive an important reply from an agency on a Friday, and the letter says a response within five days is required. You work all weekend to meet that deadline, and then you wait another month or two before you hear from the agency again. I suggest you do what they do. Somewhere in your letter state that you must hear from them within five days. In about 75 percent of the cases, you will!

Another way to get a quick response is to tell the bureaucrat in your letter that you realize how busy he is, and therefore no reply is required if he concurs with the contents of your letter. State that if no reply is received within 5 or 10 days after the date of your letter, you will assume that he agrees with your proposal. This often elicits an immediate response, especially if you send the letter by registered or certified mail.

3. Avoid calling bureaucrats on the telephone unless you know them personally from past business relationships. I once received a letter from a bureaucrat who advised me to contact him "via telephonic communication." I didn't know how to do that, so I called him on the telephone. (I was lucky because that's what he meant.) We had a lengthy and detailed conversation, and I recorded the outcome of our negotiations for my own use. I did not include additional information in my final letter—it hadn't been requested. I lost the contract. Later, he insisted he had advised me to provide the information, but I knew he hadn't. Even when I showed him

my notes from our conversation, he simply said I had forgotten, and walked away.

Always send a typed copy of the notes you take during any conversation, and request that the person you are dealing with verify your notes before you act on them. Bureaucrats understand this type of procedure and respond to it. Few of them will respond officially to a verbal agreement, so they will understand if you are reluctant to do so as well.

4. Before you deal with any bureaucrat, check carefully to be sure that he has the authority to deal with you. You may be instructed—in writing—by Mrs. X to do something concerning a contract or job, and then find out that Mrs. X had no authority to tell you to do that. As a result, you may lose your contract or get into a long, difficult, and painful negotiation. You won't be paid until you exchange many letters, attend difficult meetings, and are told how dumb you are to have followed "unauthorized orders." It is up to you to find out right at the start if the bureaucrat with whom you are dealing is authorized to deal with you, even at the risk of offending him.

5. Another way to protect yourself is to deal indirectly with bureaucrats, by using an intermediary. Then, if you make a mistake, you can immediately claim that your intermediary exceeded his authority, that he had no right to commit your company to the agreement in question. Once again, you will be pleasantly surprised to see how often bureaucrats will accept this and will let you revise, readjust, resubmit, and correct your arrangements. It can really save you a lot of trouble.

As an example, a year after we completed a job, the client's auditors consulted with one of our officials and concluded that we owed them $80,000 in unused computer time. Our official had sent a letter to the client's auditors in an attempt to explain the costs and charges. His letter was open to several interpretations, and the interpretation the client chose led to a request for reimbursement. Their whole case rested on our official's letter. I wrote a letter stating that only the president of our company was authorized to negotiate in behalf of the company, and our official had exceeded his authority; thus his letter was not an official company letter, and could not be used as such by the client. The client accepted this, since this is how bureaucracies work, and we retained the $80,000 in question.

6. Whenever you call a senior bureaucrat, you will have to speak to several subordinates, explain why you called, be put on "hold," and then start it all over again. Eventually, you will be told that the person you want is in conference and you should call back. (Many times he's in conference with a cup of coffee.) Did you ever try to speak to a bureaucrat on the telephone around 10:00 A.M. or 3:00 P.M.? They are as difficult to get hold of as a doctor on a Wednesday.

When you are expecting a bureaucrat to call, tell your secretary to advise him that you are talking to the White House, and you will return the call when you finish talking to the President. If lying bothers you, then call up the president of your school's PTA, if he lives in a white house, chat with him for a few minutes, then call the bureaucrat back and watch the reaction. If the bureaucrat asks if you were really talking to the White House, say "Yes, but the subject is classified and I'm unable to discuss it." Suggest that he forgets knowing about the conversation. The bureaucrat will raise his estimation of the level of your importance several notches. Bureaucrats really like to deal with people who know "higher ups," or who know secrets. I don't know why, but they do, so always try to give the impression that you know much more than the topic or subject at hand.

During World War II, I enlisted in the Navy. After a year, I applied for training as a naval aviator and a commission, passed the tests, and was called before a selection board of officers for an interview. After an hour of questions and answers, I was told to leave. On my way to the door, one of the officers asked me if I was related to Admiral Delany (an American Admiral with the British fleet in the Indian Ocean). I'm not related to any Admiral, but I felt that whether or not I was related to an admiral should have no bearing on my selection to enter pilot training, and I considered it to be an improper question to ask. I believed then, and I still do, that anyone who asks you a question he has no right to ask does not deserve a proper response. I couldn't say "None of your damn business" to a selection board of officers, so (rationalizing my answer by considering us all to be descendents of Adam and Eve) I said "Yes," and left the room. I was one of three men selected from my base to enter pilot training, and many, many others were not selected: who knows why?

7. In negotiating with bureaucrats, *never* accept the first offer. If you do, they will lower it. It is an automatic, knee-jerk action. You may already be the low bidder, but your quick acceptance almost always results in a reopening of negotiations. The bureaucrat will assume that you are hungry for the job, or that your price is far above what you will actually accept, or that you are not qualified to do the job, because no one else reacted the way you did. In such situations, you will probably be called in again for renegotiations and you will be given a lower price, or a request for additional work at no price increase.

Several years ago, we had a contract to provide services to a government agency. As the end of the year approached, I asked if the procuring officers wanted to negotiate for another year's service. They did, but I let time slip by. It takes the bureaucracy approximately 90 days to do anything, so when less than three months remained before the end of the first contract, I tried several times to get down to negotiations. When we were down to about two weeks before the end date, the procuring officer finally met with me. I had most of our people working on that job and we needed the new contract, so he began to negotiate from a very strong position. He said if I didn't come to terms right then and there, he would adjourn the meeting and let the contract run out. He knew I couldn't find jobs for 25 people in two weeks. I had to take a reduced fee for the second year's work and low salary increases for our people. I lost that time, but I learned from it. You win some and you lose some, but never repeat the same mistake.

8. Always let the bureaucrat lower your initial price somewhat, because he has to show his superiors that he is doing his job. Several years ago, we submitted a bid for a job, and the bureaucrat who was assigned to negotiate kept insisting that we lower our original price. Regulations require that the contract be awarded to the lowest priced responsible bidder. We had submitted a good technical proposal. Our cost structure was very low and I assumed we were the lowest bidder. But the bureaucrat wouldn't accept my first quote. He insisted that we submit a "final offer." Exasperated, I submitted a final offer in which I raised the price. The reaction was startling. I was called to a meeting with the negotiator and his two superiors. They said they had never received a final offer like that before and asked if I would agree to my initial offer. I said "No, you wanted a final offer and you got it." I won the contract, but it wasn't worth it! I earned an enemy for life in the bureaucracy. Even though I acted well within my rights, I made him look bad to his peers and superiors. Word was passed around to watch out for me, and there are more of them than there are of me.

9. The bureaucracy never makes mistakes—at least, it never admits to making any. If you and I make a mistake, then we write a follow-up letter to identify our error, apologize, and take whatever corrective action is required. But if an error emanates from the bureaucracy and you notify the bureaucrats involved, you'll hear only a thundering silence. You won't get bureaucrats to admit there is a problem (*especially* if it's serious or important). They'll just sit tight and ignore you, in hopes you will get tired and go away. This ploy works for them in about 80 percent of the cases and they know it. If you have the time, money, resources, and intestinal fortitude to persist in tracking down an error, the best you can hope for is to be told that, "It appears that an oversight [or omission or misunderstanding] has occurred." The bureaucracy will not take the blame

for an omission or oversight. Such things merely "occur," like some unfortunate but unavoidable natural disaster.

I strongly recommend against trying to prove the bureaucracy wrong or attempting to get bureaucrats to admit to an error. But if you do decide to "buck the system" you must be 100 percent right. You must have legal, financial, and support services of a very high order available, because the bureaucracy has such services at its beck and call. If what you are trying to prove may hurt a bureaucrat's reputation or chances for career advancement, everyone within the bureaucracy will unite to fight the challenge. In that way, each bureaucrat secures the support of the bureaucracy should he ever get into a similar jam.

If the foregoing examples appear to contradict one another, that's because they do. The bureaucracy is not always logical or correct. It doesn't have to be. When you find out what works for Bureaucracy A, B, or C, use it; don't worry that it doesn't make sense. If your method gets the results you want, that's what matters.

You can't fight a bureaucracy unless you use *its* rules, procedures, and methods to present your side. Watch what bureaucrats do, note how they behave and react, and do the same thing. Recent U.S. Presidents have stated publicly that they were going to make the federal bureaucracy more efficient, less wasteful, and more responsible to the public that pays for it and that it is supposed to serve. Have you observed any changes for the better? If you have, please tell me more. If the President of the United States can't change the nature of the bureaucracy, do you think you can? You don't have a chance! Even when you win an occasional small victory, as we did, you still lose more than you could ever gain.

8

Mergers and Acquisitions

(Be careful)

As small business ventures succeed and start to grow, the question of acquisitions or mergers will eventually come up for consideration. It may be in your original company plan to build your new venture to a certain size, seek the proper merger, retire, and live the life of a wealthy country squire on a lovely estate, complete with pipe, dog, and expensive tweed jackets with elbow patches. It makes for nice dreaming on a rainy Friday afternoon, but it rarely happens that way. Life, at times, can be perverse.

The union of two companies is, in many respects, like a marriage, only far more complicated. Instead of just two people adjusting to and trying to cope with each other, the merger and acquisition process involves many people, so it is even more difficult and complex. No matter how well you carry it off, someone will be unhappy about it. Business books and lectures claim that the ideal merger and acquisition process results in "synergism." That's a fancy way of saying that $2 + 2 = 6$. In other words, the combined operation is able to perform better than either of the original companies could have performed alone, so the merger or acquisition results in each participant getting more than either of them could have achieved alone. This sounds great, and so does the perfect marriage. If you know of a perfect marriage or, better still, are part of one, congratulations—you are a statistical anomaly. The same is true for synergistic mergers. Unfortunately, as with most other types of business relationships, one party generally gets more from the association than the others.

In October 1979 I attended a two-day seminar on mergers and acquisitions that was given at a local university. I wanted to learn about the mechanics of arranging a merger or acquisition because I have been approached several times by larger companies that were interested in acquiring my company. The seminar was filled with graphs, charts, pro forma P&L and balance sheets, 10-year projected earnings, projected price/earnings ratios, and all of the other numbers so dear to the hearts of accountants. What was missing was an explanation of how it all gets started. How do you decide on a price for a company? What do you do with two company presidents, two sets of officers, and two boards of directors? These, to me, are the questions of prime importance.

One of the lecturers said to pay no more than twice the book value for any company. At lunch, I sat with him and found out that he had sold a 20 percent interest in his consulting firm for five times the book value. Apparently, the buyer hadn't heard that rule. It all comes down to getting the most you can. Let me tell you about my personal experiences with mergers and acquisitions.

The first was a company in the same line of business as our company (computer software). It was a California-based operation that was buying up as many small software companies as it could in an effort to become a large, federated, national organization. It wanted us to become part of its organization, and offered unregistered stock as payment. The stock was not negotiable in the open market, and although the price was good, we wouldn't be able to sell or transfer the stock to anyone for at least three years. We refused the offer, and within the three-year period that company went out of the software business. Its stock went from $30 per share to less than $1.

The next situation was a medium-size manufacturing company that wanted to use our capability in software to enhance its newly automated hardware and to service customers. We attended several meetings at this company's corporate headquarters. It was most impressive. Everything was first class, and obviously very expensive (too expensive for my taste). The company's managers offered us unregistered stock that they said was worth $40 per share. They presented a slide show and flashed up on the screen a graph showing projected stock prices going up to $160 per share in just four years. According to them, it was clear and obvious that if we accepted their stock and joined them, within four short years the stock price would quadruple. When I asked how they knew that, the reply was, "Just look at the projections on the screen." I'm no stock market expert, but that was enough for me! I got up and left. Within that four-year period, the entire operation went into bankruptcy.

In the third case, the president of a small company was in town from Philadelphia to attend a technical seminar. He heard our named mentioned somewhere at the meetings, so he called and asked to see me. He was in the software business too, and he wanted us to merge with his company. We would retain 40 percent of the joint venture, with him in charge. I asked what his current sales and profit were. He replied with a projection of what they were going to be in three years. (Beware of people who reply to your question with a different answer, or another question.) I asked the same question again and, once again, he gave the same response. Finally I said "How many people do you have on your payroll right now?" From his answer, it was clear that his company was approximately half the size of ours; he wanted 60 percent of a joint venture to which his assets and sales would contribute 33 percent. I told him I admired his gall as I escorted him from my office.

When anyone approaches you, beware. Many people aren't in search of synergism or anything remotely connected with such goals. They are out to make a quick killing and your company or any other like it will do just fine. When a hungry tiger is on the prowl and you happen to walk by, you're in for an interesting lunch hour.

Only half of acquiring a business is buying it—the other half is what you do afterward. Many people don't look beyond the negotiations of acquiring an operation. No wonder so many mergers fail to live up to expectations. That's like getting married without planning beyond the wedding day. No matter how much money you are going to be paid for your company, keep in mind the following:

1. You will lose operating control of your company. No outfit needs two presidents. Officers of the acquired company usually leave (voluntarily or involuntarily) the new operation within 18 months after the acquisition. So don't plan on working very long in the new, post-merger setup.

2. If the price you are to be paid for your operation is dependent upon future, post-merger earnings or upon some other criteria and you are no longer in charge, you could lose everything. If an organization wants to buy your company, that's one thing. If it wants you as an employee, that's another. Don't mix them up in a combined deal, in which unforeseen post-merger problems could retroactively push the price of purchase downward. What if there is a recession? What if you became ill? Those things sometimes happen at the most unexpected and inconvenient times.

3. Be sure that what you are paid with is negotiable at your discretion. Otherwise, if things go wrong you'll sit helplessly by and watch your paper fortune dwindle down to zero. If the acquiring company is not a very large corporation, it is possible that your decision to sell a large block of your stock could drive its price down.

4. Get the best legal and accounting services you can to represent your interests prior to and during the negotiations. There are

so many ways to be paid and so many advantages, disadvantages, pitfalls, tax situations, and so on that you will need all of the help you can get.

5. Your professional relationship with your co-workers will change after the merger. You will no longer be the top man. Don't be surprised if subordinates who were formerly very cooperative and pleasant have no time for you anymore. To put it bluntly, you are no longer that important to them, or their career goals. They know you will be leaving in a year or less, anyway, so who needs a "lame duck" boss?

6. Be prepared for a number of resignations from your staff. Many people become very upset in a merger and don't stay around long enough to see what is going to happen. Since these people are probably part of the reason why you are so successful, it's only fair that you give some prior consideration to their interests, desires, and goals. Don't abandon them. Some may clearly need your leadership and support. If you want to be sure that certain key people remain, sharing a small amount of your stock or the cash received for the sale will work wonders. You can arrange a three- or four-year payout, and in such cases few people will leave—they have too much to lose, if they do.

In summary, if you are being acquired by another firm, your responsibility doesn't end on the day of the deal. Be prepared to leave very soon afterward; you may want to go or may have to go. Make sure the selling price cannot change after the sale, no matter what happens. If your stock is not negotiable, then hope for the best. In general, the larger the company that acquires you, the better your chances of making a good deal, because the stock or cash you will receive isn't personally owned by those who acquire your operation. When the stock or cash you get comes from the personal account of the president or officers of the acquiring company, much less is given up front. The principals will drive a harder bargain, and why not? Be prepared for a big cut in salary and the loss of many of the "perks" you have probably taken for granted, such as use of a company car, an expense account, and flexible hours. You'll have to account for your time spent at work; be ready to explain whom you saw, why, how often, and so on. Suddenly having a boss, after so many years of being the top person, requires an adjustment in thinking and behavior that many executives have diffiulty making. In short, you can't do it your way anymore. You are now "just another employee' in the new firm.

Many mergers are the result of "hunches," intuition, "gut feelings," and other unbusinesslike criteria. At one place I worked, our company considered acquiring a much smaller firm that produced computer equipment. A report had to be prepared for the merger/acquisitions committee to justify the venture. I was assigned the task of reporting on the company's software capability. After investigating their operation, I stated that they had no software experience or capability at all and recommended that we not acquire the company. My boss called me in and said it was already decided to buy that company and my report was the only negative one they had. He advised me to "edit" the report and make no recommendation. Our company bought the smaller firm, and it worked out great. Someone's intuition was correct.

I read about the merger of two companies with combined assets of hundreds of millions of dollars, in which both company presidents met for dinner to celebrate the forthcoming formal signing of the merger agreement. The dinner was at the home of the president of the acquiring company. The presidents and their wives were enjoying pre-dinner drinks when the host's dog bit the visiting president on the ankle. You guessed it, the merger was called off. So much for synergism and the scientific approach. (I'll bet that dog never heard of synergism.)

For every seller there has to be a buyer, so let's discuss what to look for if you acquire one or several small enterprises to add to your growing corporate structure.

1. In general (but not always), when a company is receptive to an offer to sell, it tends not to be in the best shape. There may be

a hidden or obvious problem or situation that will require your immediate attention. Carefully check the officers and the company's reputation with clients, creditors, banks, and so on. Try to ascertain how much additional cash will be required to integrate a firm into your operations. The problem of additional unexpected cash requirements after the merger is quite common.

2. Carefully plan beforehand how you will use the organization. Is it going to be a wholly owned and semi-independent subsidiary, are you going to bring it right into your organization as a division, or are you going to break it up and reorganize your operation to accommodate it? If the last alternative is in your plans, you will need many months to plan for it and you will assume the greatest risk of failure (there's too much post-merger change).

3. If you pay stock to the owners of the company you acquire, be careful to retain a voting majority. It would be most unpleasant to spend several years masterminding a series of very successful acquisitions, and then suddenly be confronted by a united group of minority stockholders whose combined ownership can outvote you. It's hard to imagine a sharp, successful, and clever entrepreneur ever letting that occur, but it has happened. In the pursuit, acquisition, and integration of company after company into a corporate empire, you may lose track of how much stock you have paid out. The unexpected realization that you have become a minority owner is a bitter pill to swallow.

4. Don't plan on using the principals of the acquired company for any important post-merger operations, and don't make any long-range plans for them. Generally, "bought" executives don't last long in the new setup. As stated earlier, statistics indicate that within 18 months they will leave for one reason or another. Some officers of the acquired company may be unwilling or unable to accept you as their new boss. You may hear things such as, "That's not the way we did it before." Of course not, but you are in charge now and you want to do things your way. You'll encounter reluctance, resistance, and outright disobedience. It is very difficult for

people who have been successful on their own to suddenly become the willing and supportive subordinate or assistant to another person. He is going to second-guess you, and you should be prepared for it.

If you bring in the new company as a semi-independent subsidiary that is not integrated into your current operations, then the top person in the new operation should be from your operation, not from the firm you acquired. Use the president of the acquired firm as an assistant or adviser to the person you place in charge. Your person knows you and relates to you; the old company president does not, and he may take one look at you and decide that he is better qualified to be "top dog" than you. And he may be very brave and forthright in saying so right to your face, even in front of others. So be careful.

5. Unexpected resignations from the staff of the newly acquired company can follow a merger. This is especially true in a service organization in which the senior staff members are highly educated and intelligent people who can easily get a new job elsewhere if the new reorganization upsets or confuses them. You can minimize this problem by meeting with the new staff before the merger, if possible, and explaining what you are going to do, why, how they fit in, and how their careers will profit from the merger. Some sellers may not allow you to do this. If the merger should fall through at the last minute, the company president would be left with a very difficult problem with the staff. (I would not allow anyone to speak to our staff about a merger, because it can be upsetting, but others may not feel this way.)

6. There very likely will be heavy demands for cash as you integrate the new operation into your corporate system. This is a very common post-merger problem that is often not anticipated. If you didn't do enough pre-merger study of the company you acquired, you'll find out about its liabilities long after its assets have been recorded on the balance sheet. Every rose has its thorns, so *caveat emptor*.

Mergers and acquisitions, if well done, can and do benefit all concerned. However, in many cases one side gains more than the other. Successful, profitable mergers get into the newspapers and business magazines, but you have to dig to find out about those that didn't work out. Naturally, anyone involved in an unsuccessful or disastrous merger will be very reluctant to discuss it openly, to admit to exercising poor judgment. Few of us want our mistakes publicized.

If you plan to buy or sell, then your viewpoint and interest will be on the side you represent. That is, of course, as it should be. If you think about what the other side wants and hopes to gain, you will be better prepared to successfully pursue your interest. Whichever side you are on, good luck to you—you will need every bit of luck you can muster for the occasion.

This is no field for amateurs, and even the "old pros" have many scars of combat in this very alluring, dangerous, and rewarding game. If your business venture is going to be acquired, the safest bet you can make, in advance, is to assume that all you will end up with is what you receive for the sale of your company on "day one."

As said earlier, 50 percent of the work remains to be done after the merger takes place. Very careful advance planning is required by both sides, but especially by the buyer. He has to make it work afterward. The seller is now under his direction and control. If the seller gets what he wanted from the deal, he may not care very much about the direction of the operation, or he may care too much. Even though he has sold his "baby," he may still feel it in some way belongs to him.

A successful artist was barred from art exhibits because he had, on several occasions, brought his paints and brushes to galleries in which some of his paintings were on display. Even though they had been sold years before to collectors, the artist still felt they were "his," and he would go in and "touch them up a bit," when the spirit moved him. The paintings were no longer his property; however, he felt that they were his creations, no matter who owned them. If you feel that way about your corporate creation, then don't sell it. If you sell it, and you feel like the artist did about his creations, then you're in for trouble.

You may now be able to better understand why the executives of the acquired companies tend, on average, to be all gone within 18 months or so after the merger. Some lose interest then, because they have their nest egg, and others retain too much interest, and they interfere with and resist the necessary changes that must happen after the merger takes place. They want to keep "touching up" the picture as they did in the past, when they owned and had complete control over it.

9

Going Public

Shares in a corporation can be sold privately or publicly. If you choose to sell shares to the general public via the stock market, you are in for a long, tedious, and possibly risky affair. "Going public" is the typical way in which the growing small business venture comes of age. If you go that route you'll find out what you are worth in the marketplace. Many imponderable factors will affect the price of your stock and thus the real value of the shares you own. Recession, inflation, war, the economic policy of the government, and even foreign nations can and will affect the price of any stock on the open market.

Rumors about you and your company will be circulated. Whether they're true or not, your stock's value will fluctuate as the general public buys or sells your stock in its reaction to what it thinks or believes is happening. You may deny stories of impending mergers or acquisitions and swear that tales of good or bad turns in your affairs are not true, but to no avail. The fact that you discuss and deny the rumors only fuels the fire. Why would any company open itself up to such goings on? Because it's one of the best and quickest ways to become rich. There are other ways, such as the sale of your company to a larger company, but you have the opportunity to gain (or lose) much more by going public.

The advantages of a public vs. a private offering of your stock are several. First, with many hundreds of separate owners of your stock you can sell a higher percentage of your company, even majority shares, yet still retain voting control by retaining a large block of minority shares. If you sell a large portion of your company's stock at a private offering to a small group, they are much more likely to try to exert some management control over your company. They will, very likely, put their own representatives on your board of directors to look after their investments, and why not? The investment may be substantial. Another advantage of going public is that you are likely to receive more money in a general offering than in a private sale. This is not *always* true; it depends on the brokerage house that takes you public and on the business arrangements you make. General economic conditions can have a good or bad effect on stock sold publicly, but do not affect privately held shares as much. Don't go public during a period of recession, when the stock market is experiencing a downturn. Those who bought stock via a private sale tend to know more about you and your company—outside economic conditions affect them less than the conditions affect public shareholders.

Once again, you will need expert legal and accounting advice, and your company lawyer or CPA may not be experienced or qualified to handle this very specialized area of business. A mistake at this stage of the game can really put a crimp in your plans and can even wipe out the effort that brought your successful small venture to the edge of the public marketplace. Be certain that your advisers are operating in your company's interest, and are not looking for a nice fee for a temporary, relatively short-term job. Paying them in stock rather than the high fees they command is one very good way to help assure their total and long-range interest in your public offering. Perhaps a combination of a low fee and stock would be more agreeable or acceptable. If the experts insist on cash regardless of what happens, then I suggest you rethink your public offering if you can, because this means that even your legal and CPA advisers, who must know a great deal about your company, do not want the stock you are going to try to sell in the open market. If they don't want it, why should others want it? Think about that.

If you elect to go public, you will have to find a brokerage firm that will handle your sale of stock. The larger and most reputable houses probably won't take you public. Most won't handle anything less than a multi-million-dollar operation and shy away from first or second public offerings of small companies.

In looking for a smaller firm you'll need careful legal advice. Check out the firms you are considering very carefully. Have they been in business for a long time? Have they switched operations from state to state, periodically, and, if so, why? Request and study the records of other companies they have taken public. Contact the corporate offices of their clients and see what they have to say. Don't hurry, no matter what anyone says. Remember, you will be committing your dearly loved company into the hands of others now, and they may not love it or care about it to the same degree that you and your principals do. You can't expect them to, can you? You are just another corporate body coming down the hall for the financial doctors to work on. Some live, some die, but the line rolls on down the hall, and your long-term corporate health and survival may be of little or no interest to the broker who takes you public. He gets his (very large) fee right up front, and some may quickly lose interest in you after this first brief encounter.

Now you come in contact with the Securities and Exchange Commission (SEC). This agency's job is to look out for and protect the interest of public investors. Before the SEC came on the scene, the raping and pillaging that went on would make Ivan the Terrible look like a boy scout at a church picnic. You will have to comply with every single SEC rule and regulation, and don't play games here. People can be put in jail for violating SEC rules. You aren't going to break any SEC rules deliberately, I am sure, but don't break any due to an oversight or to your ignorance of the law. Remember, ignorance of the law is no excuse and you don't need the legal hassles or fines for inadvertent violations of SEC regulations. This hurts any corporation at any time. With your small venture, it could be deadly. Who wants to buy the stock of a small company that is in some sort of "hot water" with the SEC?

Let's get into some specifics.

1. You have to prepare a prospectus in which you announce what you plan to use the money for when you sell the stock. This is a very important document, so turn it over to your legal and financial adviser, but be sure it is explained to you, word by word, because it's your responsibility to carry out what you put in the prospectus. Do this correctly and well. If you later use the funds for reasons other than those listed in your prospectus, stand by for a stockholder suit and a game of "20 questions" with the SEC.

2. You will be required to prepare and issue an annual report. This report will contain your salary and perks and the same information about all corporate officers. It's all public information now.

3. You will be required to hold annual stockholders meetings at which you must account for salaries and dividends. You may not enjoy this annual inquisition at all, but it's the law, and stockholders have every right to question you about "their company," because they legally own part of it. You are working for them. In recent years, some people have bought a few shares in a big or small company and have attended annual meetings to get even with the fat cats or to hassle the big boys. This can happen to you as the president or senior officer in a publicly held corporation.

4. After the company has gone public you won't be able to run the show the same way you did before, so don't try. In addition to the state and federal regulations you must obey, there are forms and reports that must be prepared and submitted, and you won't

have the freedom to "wheel and deal" as you did in the old days, when yours was a privately held company.

As chief executive officer of a publicly held company, you may be sued by shareholders for not using "wise and prudent judgment," for failure to exercise "due diligence," for self-dealing, and for negligence. You can be held personally liable for such offenses. Do you want a jury to pass judgment on your behavior and activities as the boss of an outfit because stockholders think you are wrong? A jury is more likely to empathize with the person who is suing you. You are entitled to a jury of your peers, but I doubt that the court would permit you or your lawyer to insist on a jury of company presidents.

Your potential liability now can be extended beyond your ownership in the corporation to include your personal assets. You could, of course, transfer all of your personal assets to your spouse, children, or other relatives in order to protect yourself from the potential risk, but, in such cases, you may be opening yourself up to the far greater and more immediate risk of not owning your home or other personal assets.

5. If you had a successful public offering in which you sold 25 percent of the company stock for $2 million, don't assume that the remaining 75 percent is worth $6 million. The stock market doesn't work that way. Even if the stock you sold initially for $5 per share is now up to $10, it doesn't automatically follow that the 75 percent that you have retained is worth $12 million now. You may be a millionaire on paper—the problem is how to turn it into cash. The stock that you hold is probably unregistered, and if you want to register and sell some on the open market, you have to get permission from the SEC. Let's say you do get permission to sell another 25 percent of your stock, you'll have to state what you want it for. If you want the money for your own personal use, that may be OK with the SEC, but what about the buying public? People will want to know why you are selling your own personal shares. They'll ask, "Why should I buy stock in this company when its president wants

to sell his own shares to use the money elsewhere?" Such an event could have a very negative effect upon the price you get. In a very short time, the $10 per share price could drop to $1.50 or less, and your broker will have trouble finding a buyer at all.

If several corporate officers tried to sell sizable blocks of their own stock in a short period of time, that is even worse news to the buying public. Your $10 paper stock certificates can suddenly become quite worthless.

6. You may not be able to buy your own company's stock on the open market, and for good and sufficient reasons. As an insider you know more about the future of your company than anyone else. Suppose you have just returned from very successful negotiations at which you landed a large new contract that may increase your sales and profit by 100 percent in the next year or two. Great! However, if you think you can buy company stock on the open market, release the news of the new contract, watch the stock price double, and then sell your shares in six months or so for a nice capital gain, think again. You traded on inside information and acted in your own best interests, not in the best interests of the stockholders whom you are supposed to represent, and that is illegal. It's also irresponsible. What would you think of a ship's captain who, upon receiving information that a hole has developed in the engine room, quietly gets into a lifeboat and sails away to avoid the rush that will occur when the crew and passengers become aware of the problem?

By now you are probably saying to yourself, what a mess! I can't sell my stock unless I use the money for further company growth. I can't buy it, even if I believe it's a bargain. If I try to sell any stock in large volume, I can destroy the market for everyone who owns the stock. If I want to get out and enjoy the fruits of my labor, can I do that and personally use those capital gains tax laws? These are problems for the owner/entrepreneur of the growing small business that went public. The problems are especially acute if it went public too early in the growth of the company. If you think you can have someone else—an agent or trusted business associate—buy and sell on your behalf, paying a fee of 10 percent or so, hold it right there! Don't try that one either. It may bring you right into the arms of the SEC, IRS, Justice Department, Treasury Department, and so on. You can see, now, that you'll need good legal and accounting advice as you operate a small business that has gone public.

Be very careful whom you talk to and what you say about your company. I read of a case in which the president of a small company mentioned casually to several employees that the coming year would bring vast increases in sales and profit to the company and that the price for the company stock in the open market was far too low and would soon go up. You guessed it: Some of those employees bought shares over the counter. The following year the projected sales and profit did not materialize and the stock went down in value. The employees sued the president to recover their losses. Their argument went something like this: Since the president suggested that they buy the stock, they were afraid he would get upset and fire them if they did not buy it. They claimed they were, in reality, "forced" to buy the stock. (I don't think they would have used this argument if the stock had gone up.) Be careful. You can't tout your own stock, even in casual conversations.

You may even get into difficulty in touting other companies' stock. This almost happened to me. One evening after normal working hours, when I thought I was alone in the office, I received a telephone call from a stockbroker who was trying to interest me in buying some shares of a company that was going public. I was unaware that an employee working late in another office was eavesdropping. He went home and bought several thousand dollars worth of the stock that he overheard me discussing. I didn't buy any. The company later went bankrupt. At our Christmas party, he had a few drinks too many, got up his false courage, and came straight at me. In no uncertain terms he told me that I had cost him $3,000 and explained how. I told him he had no right to listen in on my private conversations. When I told him that I did not buy the stock, he really became upset. His wife had to drag him away before he got himself fired from his job. Our company attorney later assured me that I had nothing to worry about, because of the way the information was acquired. However, had I repeated the telephone conversation to the employee after I hung up, then I might very well have been liable for his loss. My lawyer said, "Don't talk about business, yours or anyone else's. You never know how people will misconstrue or twist what you say, so stay away from these types of discussions. Stick to sports, current events, the weather, and you can't go wrong." I have tried my best to follow this advice ever since. When you are the boss, watch what you say.

How can you get rich from your own company? You can sell your own personal stock for your own gain, but do it the way your lawyer and broker advise. Do it openly. If you plan to retire, everyone will understand that. You may have to sell it off in small blocks over a period of a year or two, so that your broker can maintain an orderly market for its sale. That's possible if your departure does not give the impression of a "bail out." It is a good idea to notify the SEC in advance, explain your plans, and get its approval. If your replacement mismanages the operation and stock prices go down and stay down, the SEC may investigate to determine whether you knew about the unfortunate events that were about to occur and therefore bailed out under the guise of going into retirement. Once again, you don't need those problems at that stage of your life. You can retire, but do it by the rules.

Let's compare the life of a corporation with a long race. The first leg is a difficult obstacle course; many fail, and runners must climb over, around, and through many barriers. This is what the founding enterpreneur faces. When he gets the company through this first and most difficult part of the race, he steps aside and passes the baton to the follow-up team. Those runners have a different and easier race to run. The next leg may still be uphill, but the course is set and the road is now clear and paved, so the second president can go much faster and farther. He is starting with a growing concern, positive cash flow, customers, good employees, and a hard-earned company reputation.

Growth for the successful business is exponential. If the founder leaves early on and a new team takes over, the company can increase sales by 10, 15, or 20 million dollars within five years. In such cases, the retired entrepreneur tends to receive far less from his efforts than the follow-up team does. The best way to cope with this psychologically is to set a goal for what you want to get out of your efforts. If you reach it, don't worry about what those who came after you are making.

There is a time when you should leave, and if you don't plan for it and leave gracefully, then you will be pushed aside and you may not like how you fall. Chapter 14 discusses when and how to leave. Just as the hypothetical race changes from an obstacle course to an uphill race, to a race down a long smooth roadway, the nature of any business changes from infancy, to corporate teenager, to full maturity. Each phase calls for a different type of leadership, and you can do more harm than good by hanging around too long, telling everyone that the company never would have gotten off the ground without you. People now want to look foward, not backward. If you go public, do it carefully. Reap your well-deserved reward and then cheerfully and willingly pass on the leadership to younger, more vigorous hands, when the time comes. Take what is yours and hope that those who succeed you will do even better.

10

Delegating Authority

(You can't do it all)

A business must be properly managed. No one will argue with that, I'm sure. But what constitutes proper management? Now the differences of opinion, abilities, and interests come into play. Management involves planning, organizing, directing, and controlling an operation to accomplish its defined task or achieve its goal. It also involves proper and judicious expenditure of one's time. Lost time can never be recovered. A day wasted on the wrong job or client can never be relived. You can, of course, adjust, correct, modify, or compensate for illspent time, but you never get it back. Once it's gone, it's gone forever. So, as managers of the new small business venture, we must constantly guard against wasting time or spending it in the wrong area.

Since you now have few, if any, superiors (you always longed for this day, didn't you?), there is no one around to correct you, advise you, or redirect your efforts into more productive channels. You're the captain of the ship now, and have absolute authority over the fate of your small venture and all who sail with it. Wonderful! But what do you do on a day-to-day basis to make it succeed?

In very large companies, the various functions (engineering, administration, finance, purchasing, accounting, plant safety, security, and so on) become separate areas of responsibility. Specific people are assigned to each area, and each person is responsible for one job. He knows what it is and so does everyone else. There is little overlap in responsibility. A manager has no "pull" in areas other than his own, and does not have to decide each day where he is needed most or what job to do.

In the small business venture, one person or a small group of people must do several or all of these jobs, and this can cause confusion. If responsibilities overlap, if efforts are duplicated, if contradictory orders are given, corporate chaos soon follows. When your new venture is very small, it may be possible for you to do all or most of the required tasks, but as your business prospers and grows, you should plan to delegate authority to other competent people and thereby free yourself for more important things. As soon as you know how to do some job, look for someone else to whom you can assign the responsibility. Then work in an area where confusion and uncertainty reign supreme. Analyze the situation, reorganize procedures as necessary, and then pass responsibility on to someone else. You won't ever be bored in a job like that. You may be frightened, you'll probably make mistakes, you'll be insulted, and you'll be accused (correctly) of not knowing what you are doing—but I assure you, you won't be bored. You will always be where the important action is. Of course, you may choose to assign yourself to a nice, safe job and let others stay up front, where the real fighting is taking place. If you avoid combat or delegate it to others, you will fail, because you have then delegated your true leadership function to subordinates.

When my youngest daughter was in the third grade, one of her classmates asked her what her father did for a living. My daughter replied, "He goes to work and yells at people." I don't go to work to yell at people, and I don't "yell" very much any more, but I have to admit that nine or ten years ago I did do a lot of yelling. I was not going to sit quietly by and let people sabotage or destroy our company—not in its early years, when mistakes of any kind can be fatal. If you haven't done much yelling before, you'll find plenty to yell about after you start a new business venture. If you are now in the early stage of your new venture and find yourself yelling a lot, don't despair. It's normal and it will pass. As you grow, you can hire someone else to yell for you.

Why do some entrepreneurs fail to delegate authority and responsibility when they should? There are many reasons, but let's discuss the most typical ones.

1. The entrepreneur feels that the whole venture was his idea and becomes totally wrapped up with his "baby," to the exclusion of everything else. The overly committed entrepreneur likes to put in long hours at work. He is convinced that he is the only one who can do anything right. He must do the payroll and he must see each client or employee personally. He must handle every problem no matter how trivial. (I know, because I did this for a while.) He won't take a vacation because he doesn't trust anyone alone with the new baby. When this happens, the following usually results:

○ The company will stay small, since only one person can do anything.
○ Each day, employees will wait their turn for the boss's orders, which are communicated personally.
○ The entrepreneur is so busy with details that he has no time to handle big problems or areas of new business.
○ Home and family life suffer.
○ Personal friendships are neglected.
○ If the entrepreneur becomes ill, the company may fail before he recovers.
○ There is no second-level management for expansion or growth. The entrepreneur is not prepared to seize an unexpected opportunity.

2. A problem similar to the situation described in item 1 can exist when the entrepreneur's ego is the primary reason for the new venture. In such cases, he prides himself on knowing more about the operation than anyone else, and can actually feel threatened by some other company official or employee with new or better ideas. Instead of feeling the pride that a coach does in training his team to play and win, this ego-centered individual wants to be the star of the game who coaches when he's not playing. It can't be done. Each is a full-time job and calls for different interests, talents, and goals. Management is coaching, and the ego-centered entrepreneur who insists on being the star employee can't be a star manager. We call it the "withdrawal syndrome" when a star employee is promoted to a management position, but continues doing his old job instead of the new one. He's afraid of withdrawing from the game and losing the skills he used every day before his promotion.

When an entrepreneur displays this ego problem, it can be very serious. One of our principals behaved this way for years, and nothing anyone could say would change him. Sheer exhaustion eventually forced him to withdraw and delegate some of his work to others. He's an excellent person and a valuable member of the team, but he works too hard. I guess he wants it that way.

Other more serious and more damaging events can result. In some small operations, one person may wear two hats. He must know when to switch and when to delegate. In one case, an engineer/treasurer had no experience in finance. As his company grew, his duties as treasurer required more and more of his attention, but he stayed on his technical job. The finance reports were a mess. Money started to pile up and he didn't account for it. He left it sitting in a checking account. The amount went into six figures and drew no interest. The president hired a CPA to come in as a consultant to straighten out the corporate accounts. Instead of being happy and relieved about the help he was going to receive, the treasurer felt threatened and resisted. Instead of cooperating with the CPA, he actually sabotaged the CPA's efforts by withholding information concerning the location and amounts of corporate funds. After three months of fruitless efforts and expense, the consultant resigned and told the president about the problem. This ego-centered person was going to ruin the company because of the way he viewed his responsibilities and his involvement in the company. The situation was eventually put right, but it was a very unhappy and unnecessary affair, which affected a fine, young, growing venture.

This ego problem is not by any means restricted to small companies. It has affected even the largest companies. Ego-centered people want their own group, department, or division to succeed and shine above all others, and in their pursuit of their goals they damage other divisions or the corporate body.

I don't believe you can change people's attitudes, so the best way to deal with ego-centered individuals is to move them away from areas in which they can damage other operations. They don't belong in line management. Perhaps you can put them on a staff. They make wonderful spies, and they enjoy reporting about other divisions' inefficiencies or errors. They love to second-guess others; it makes them feel superior. They can be useful to you as investigators and advisers. Use them to get information and data, but save the decisions for yourself or other, more stable and considerate types of managers.

Don't let ego-centered people or other abrasive personalities work with your managers, staff, or clients. At one company I worked for, a highly competent project manager gave a technical progress report to the client's staff. The room was dark as he used an overhead projector to display his slides on the wall. Someone in the room asked a question. The project manager, a man with a very strong ego, replied, "Whoever asked that stupid question has paid no attention to what I have been discussing for the past hour." Of course, it was the senior member of the client's staff, the top man, who had asked the question. He rose and walked out. The project manager was replaced later that day.

3. You must guard against becoming too involved in one aspect of the job while letting other areas go unattended. You probably enjoy the type of work you did before elevation into management. If you came from a technical background, it's only natural for you to place more emphasis and time on that area of responsibility, which you understand and are comfortable with. Areas such as pricing, accounting, client relations, advertising, and government regulations will be less appealing. Don't be afraid to delegate to others, as long as you and they know what they are supposed to do, how, when, what the chain of command is, and where they should and should not act.

In delegating authority and responsibility to subordinate managers, you are, of course, taking a risk. You are permitting others to have a major impact on the success or failure of your enterprise. This is the reason why many entrepreneurs tend to hold all authority within their own hands. From a short-term viewpoint, the reasoning is difficult to refute. Bad decisions made by subordinate managers can have a devastating effect upon you, especially if you are unaware of a problem or if you find the subordinate to be working at cross-purposes to your plans or intentions.

An amusing example can prove the point. When we hired our first accountant, we gave him total responsibility for setting up a good internal accounting system. Having had little experience with accountants, I thought they were all the same. Boy, was I wrong! I had hired a bookkeeper who needed a supervisor on a daily basis. He would come to me to ask questions on accounting and my reply always was, "I don't know, that's what we hired you to do." The straw that broke the camel's back was the day he told me that our petty cash account was off by 10 cents (literally). I said, "So what? No one audits petty cash. We always carry it on the books at $50. Forget about it." Four hours later he returned to my office with a smile of triumph on his face. He had found the 10-cent error and corrected it. I asked him if he thought it was a good idea for our company to pay him for half a day's work to account for 10 cents. I now began to question his judgment on how he felt he should spend his time. He very obviously was not going to be our lead company accountant. If you delegate authority, you might consider having each manager preparing for you a written plan of objectives and responsibilities. This document can later be used as a basis for bonuses, promotions, raises, and so on. It's all based on the individual's own statements of the objectives he plans to accomplish for your company. Have it revised every six months or so to keep it current. In this way, you won't get into the affair I had with our "accountant."

Conduct the orchestra; don't play the instruments. If you need a first violinist, go hire and train one, but don't rush off the podium, grab a violin, and start playing. If you do, the concert will sound like a chorus of alley cats—even if you're playing the violin beautifully.

You will have to delegate authority. You can plan for it or do it by default. Someone else will assume the authority if you don't. Either his ego will drive him to assume all of the authority he can until someone stops him, or else someone will make decisions because they have to be made and you aren't there. Even though it's true that most people tend to be indecisive and avoid making decisions, believe me, someone down the line will do it, sooner or later. Do you want delayed decisions, or no decisions, or wrong decisions made because you were not available? If you don't, plan and organize your operation so you can clearly delegate authority along with the responsibility. Don't give anyone responsibility without authority. Both should go together.

In delegating authority, you have to first divide your organization along either project or functional lines. A project division contains all the required talent and support to do an entire job; that is, a manager, secretarial and administrative support staff, engineers, suppliers, and so on. In a functionally organized operation, secretarial or typing pools, programmers, inventory, manufacturing, and engineering are all separate specialized functions, upon which project managers draw as if each were a subcontractor.

I can't tell you how to organize your company. As you grow, your clients may be located over a wider area, and project-oriented operations may be more appropriate. At first, though, when your operation is small and located under one roof, it can be organized either way or in some combination of the two. In any case, structuring requires careful and exact planning and organizing. You must be able to direct and control operations quickly, meaningfully, on a day-by-day basis, with a minimum expenditure of time.

Clients expect small operations to respond quickly, even immediately, to sudden changes in their requirements. We all know this is not possible in the large, bureaucratic operations, so no one expects a quick response from them. One reason large companies and the government contract out for services is to ensure a rapid response to changing conditions—something they can't get from their own environment. This is especially true in areas of research and development, the leading edge of any new technology. If you are poorly organized and directed, and your company is unable to accept and respond to sudden changes in a project, you sacrifice your biggest advantage over larger companies. They are bigger. You are supposed to be faster.

If your company is well organized, it should be able to function smoothly in your absence. I have noted that whenever I am on vacation nice things happen to our company. We received two very large new contracts while I was away. I like to think that reflects our fine organizational structure and our well-trained managers and staff. (There is, of course, another obvious explanation, but my ego can't face that possibility.)

A good span of control to use is one supervisor for every five people. This is not an ironclad rule. In some cases one person can handle up to ten others quite well, but that should not be a permanent arrangement. If many jobs are filled by temporary workers, it's OK to put an acting manager in charge, but not for more than three or four months. (That's a good way to try out new supervisors. If they don't work out too well, they don't have to be demoted. When the temporary job ends, the supervisors can return to their former level with their egos intact.)

After you have structured your company along whatever organization lines you like (project, functional, or a combination of the two) and you have set up a span of control (five subordinates to one manager), you will have to direct and control the operation. That requires an internal communication system. Orders go down from above and reports come up from below. Heed this well. Especially at the start, communication tends to be much too informal. Verbal orders are subject to misunderstanding, misinterpretation, and confusion.

Like many other things, writing down your instructions, directives, plans, goals, and so on is a habit that will stand you in good stead. I have always kept a daily log in which I write down the significant events of the day. I am unable to count how many times this log book saved pointless arguments or discussions concerning dates of small or significant events in the office. When people know you maintain a log and you say that such and such is in my log book, the argument or discussion generally stops then and there, especially when others have no log or written records to support their position.

Orders, plans, and directives are sent down the chain of command in written form. What comes up? Progress reports should be submitted every week. Each employee should be required to write one every week and submit it to his or her immediate supervisor, who reads, initials, and dates it. The manager then prepares a progress report for his or her manager, at the next level, and so on. Under this arrangement, every manager has no more than five reports to read before he writes his report.

In our company, each manager must speak to everyone who is one level above and below him, every day. That way, serious problems don't have to wait until the weekly report. I strongly recommend the "management by exception technique" for progress reports. In this method, you report on what did *not* go according to plan, or on any problems that have come up or might come up. If the project is on schedule the weekly report is brief: "On schedule. No problems. Next milestone and the expected date will be met, as of this date." If, however, anything diverges from your plan (the exceptions), then a detailed explanation of the problem and proposed solutions are required.

The progress report can be written on one piece of paper. We had to restrict the length of the weekly reports, because of an unfortunate human quirk. The less we know about something, the more we tend to write or talk about it. (If you don't believe me, ask any teacher or professor.) People seem to think that if they don't know an answer, they should put down everything they can possibly think of that is in any way related to the question at hand, in hopes of diverting the reader from what he wants to know. Keep this in mind when you read progress reports and work schedules for projects, then look for what is not reported, but should be. If a schedule milestone was supposed to have been completed on Monday and it is not reported upon, then ask about it. "Oh it was done on Thursday, and I forgot to put the date in my progress report." You just uncovered a three-day slippage on the task, which may or may not be important. If slippages like that occur *every* week, you may end up with a 30-day or even greater overrun. Remember, no one likes to write down that he is behind schedule, is in some difficulty, or needs help. It's up to the manager to monitor the progress and decide if, when, and how to intervene. Without the written progress report you will have to do a lot of running around, talking, and yelling.

If I have convinced you of the joys of corporate organization, of establishing levels of authority and responsibility, great. But don't go overboard. An unnecessary level of command is costly and wasteful. I know of one company with 15 employees and seven levels of management. I don't think there are that many levels in an army division. The president had read a book on managing a large company, and tried to become a big company by imitating the structure of one. That's like trying to become a great painter by cutting off your ear. A little common sense is needed. If you are in any doubt as to whether or not you need a new level of authority, it's always best to wait. You can always set one up, but it's very difficult to take one away. Remember, people have egos.

I hope I have convinced you that you can't do it all. You should be ready, willing, and able to delegate authority, so you can back off from day-to-day problems and spend your valuable time and efforts on things that are more important. As the top person, you should be concerned with the future; with new work, new equipment, sources of funds for capital expansion, and so on. If you tie yourself into the day-to-day problems, you won't have the time, energy, or inclination to handle long-range projects. It's your outfit and it's up to you to decide what you do with your time and what you want in return for your efforts. You'll have to delegate sooner or later, and it's better to do it by your plan and your schedule than by anyone else's.

11

Indecision

Webster's Third New International Dictionary defines indecision as an "... inability or failure to arrive at a decision; vacillation." It doesn't sound too bad, but the general consensus of opinion of senior personnel seems to be that this one problem has wrecked more careers than any other single personality characteristic. Some people who have risen to the top in their chosen careers have been smart and others have not been so smart. Good-looking people have made it, but so have unattractive people. People have topped out who were charming, and others with the personality of a trapped bear have done well too. Honest people have risen to the top; dishonest people have risen to the top. Hard workers have achieved success, but so have those who didn't work hard but rode on the careers of others. Yes-men have made it, and free thinkers have too.

Successful people don't necessarily have much in common with one another in the way of personal characteristics, intelligence, honesty, morality, physical appearance, and so on. But there is something that these diverse, successful people share that seems to give them the edge over others. They are decisive. They will make decisions and they aren't afraid to take risks. When it's time to do something, they do it. Others stand around and wait for someone else to act. Napoleon, when asked what single characteristic he thought was most important in his generals, said, "I like lucky ones." I believe Napoleon meant that the risk-taker who wins more than he loses is preferable to the military tactician or strategist who waits for more information before he acts. By waiting, he loses the opportunity and usually has enough information to make his decision when it's too late to matter. We rarely, if ever, have all of the information we want or need. Somewhere along the line one must decide what to do—when the time has come, the time has come. History is full of stories and records of people who did great things and achieved great goals by making gutsy decisions. The decision maker acts and then stands ready to pay the consequences, one way or the other.

Most of us will probably never find ourselves in earthshaking situations, but is there a message coming through or a lesson to be learned that can help us? I think so. I sent a questionnaire to one hundred senior executives in business. Question 38 on the survey was: "What single factor do you consider most significant in preventing subordinates from rising higher in your organization?" Sixty-five percent of the respondents said, *indecisiveness*.

Why are people afraid to make decisions? Perhaps they are afraid of the unknown or, worse, of making a mistake and being proved wrong. Fear of change per se could be another factor to inhibit them. (That's fear of the unknown again.) I guess most people want security. If we face up to the fact that there is no security this side of the grave and that we must take risks and make decisions in order to do anything well, then decision making might come easier.

I don't think there is much that anyone can do one way or the other about a person who lacks the ability to make decisions. We can train just about any willing person with reasonable intelligence to do most jobs. Intellectual ability or lack of it seldom seems to be the problem in limiting one's advancement. Indecision seems to be a built-in emotional response to unusual or unexpected situations. In fact, in many cases the indecisive person is unaware that he is indecisive. People who vacillate can be very creative in coming up with reasons why they couldn't make a decision when one was due.

Any good manager or supervisor will tell you that the place he is needed most is where the problems are or the action is. In football, the middle linebacker or free safety follows the action and reacts to the situation as it unfolds before him. You cannot train anyone to do this. He just knows when to rush in and when to drop back to anticipate the pass. He must anticipate, decide, and act— because if he waits to see where the ball goes before he makes his move, then it is too late. Coaches will tell you it is hard, if not impossible, to teach this sort of thing. You can teach a man how to be a quarterback, but not how to anticipate.

Decisive people can and do make mistakes. In fact, they make more mistakes than other people because they make more decisions than others. It's possible for a decision maker to be unintelligent, to lack ability or judgment. In an organization, such a person can really mix up the works, because most of the time he is wrong (or, if you prefer, unlucky). They are quite rare, but when identified they should be removed as soon as possible; you can't stop them from making decisions. It is possible to never encounter this kind of person in one's career, but be aware that they are around. They can pull down the careers of others around them.

You are most likely to encounter the hard-working, intelligent, dedicated subordinates or superiors who do their job and deserve some advancement, but tend to be indecisive. When given the next higher position, they start to "drop the ball" because the job calls for decisions and they just don't make them in time, or at all. They are probably very conservative and cautious. Since they don't make decisions, things happen *to* them; other people make decisions for them. They spend their time reacting to events rather than acting and controlling the events. It is sad to watch. They get hit over and over again and they don't know why. A person may have the education, training, experience, and ability to function in a decision-making capacity, but nevertheless things can go wrong; schedules slip, cost overruns occur, and so on. It never seems to be entirely the manager's fault, but things just do not work out. The "chemistry" isn't there. It's up to higher management to replace such a manager quickly.

Only about 10 percent of any typical group of people have the ability and desire to exercise decision-making authority. In the smaller organization, it is easy to spot those who make decisions and those who don't. But in the larger organizations, they are more difficult to identify and their effects can be much more serious and far-reaching. Things happen or fail to happen, and no one knows who authorized or failed to authorize activities. When decisions and plans haven't been made, it shows, up and down the line.

When I was in my early twenties, I worked in an organization that was directed and run by the manager's secretary, who was considerably more decisive than her boss. She made all the decisions through him, and influenced his opinions. She became progressively more confident, bold, and open about it, and although she was effective and performed her boss's job for him rather well, she alienated and offended people in the organization. If she had developed some tact, she could have continued to run the company, but she lost out in the power struggle because she forgot that most people saw her as a secretary who had no business being actively involved in the decision-making process. She eventually left the company.

The situation was the fault of the boss. He was a nice guy who wouldn't hurt anyone, but his indecisiveness resulted in hurt feelings, transfers, arguments, and other unfortunate reactions that could have been avoided. Nature and organizations abhor a vacuum. Someone will exercise the authority inherent in any group. If leadership is not exercised by the top man, someone else down the line will exercise it for him, with or without his knowledge.

Even though you can't change the nature of an indecisive person, you must deal with him in some way. If you are placed below such a person in your organization, he can slow up your career advancement. The group to which you belong won't perform well in the long run, and everyone associated with a loser suffers. If one of your subordinates is indecisive, he too can inhibit or arrest your career advancement. As the senior manager, you are accountable for your subordinates' failures and achievements. Subordinates who vacillate will tend to require a disproportionate amount of your time. They'll look up, down, and sideways for some help when it comes time to make a decision. You can observe, measure, and study the symptoms and progress of this illness, and can predict with a fair degree of accuracy the ultimate conclusion.

It is my opinion that chronic indecision is an incurable ailment. Let's look at the symptoms and prognosis. Indecisive people tend to imitate others, even so far as to dress like managers whom they admire. When asked why they do things in a certain way, they will often respond by saying, "So-and-so does it this way." They don't want to do it their own way—that may be different and they don't want to be different.

A decisive person makes both personal and career plans. People who don't plan their work and actively direct its progress are showing one of the classic signs of indecision. If you don't know what is going on or what you're supposed to do, then you can't be expected to make decisions, can you? In order to make decisions, you have to have some sort of plan or goal; otherwise, on what basis are the decisions to be made? How do you judge success or failure? A decisive person is not afraid to take a risk or to seek change. Some even enjoy it, for it can be exciting at times. When the time comes to decide he decides. It's that simple.

The decision maker is not afraid to put his decisions on record for later judgment or evaluation. If a person always wants to know first what you think and rarely tells you what he thinks, then look out. During the Civil War, President Lincoln had to find a new commander for the Union Army. (He was having trouble with indecisive Army commanders back then.) Mr. Lincoln presented the name of his choice for the new commander to the cabinet for discussion. After much debate, he called for a vote. The 12 cabinet members voted "no." Mr. Lincoln announced the results of the ballot. He said 12 "no's" and one "aye"; the "aye's" have it. Mr. Lincoln, who voted yes, was telling his cabinet members that their votes were advisory only. He was the decision maker, and he wasn't afraid to do it his way.

Superiors, peers, or subordinates who continually form or join committees and let the committees run things may be indecisive. Committees should not be given decision-making power, except under very unusual and temporary circumstances. Committees are most useful when they collect information and serve as advisers to the decision makers. In a small business, committees should be avoided like the plague.

If you are indecisive by nature, then don't become an entrepreneur (see Chapter 1). You have the wrong type of personality for leading a small business venture. You may do well in a large bureaucratic organization, in which you will have to make few major decisions. In a bureaucracy, you will have to read, interpret, and apply the big book of regulations. In most situations, you won't really make decisions, you will apply the decisions that others have made for you. If the situation under review is not in the book, you'll probably refer the case up the line rather than decide for yourself.

If you aren't a decisive leader, your small business won't last long enough to have the problems that accompany growth or expansion. If you are decisive, your operation will take off. As you expand and hire new senior staff, you must carefully choose your subordinate managers. Managers who come from large organizations tend to be indecisive, and if you hire one you may have to fit a round peg in a square hole in your operation. Since most small new ventures have few or no formal policies and procedures, no rulebook to guide middle managers, you have to let them use their judgment and make decisions. In most situations, the worst decision of all is no decision.

I believe the problem of indecision is so common in organizations of all sizes, that it merits special attention. Indecision damages or interrupts many careers. As the leader of the small company, you have to be careful—you don't want an indecisive person to pull the whole thing down around your ears. In addition to damaging himself, he can, in the small business operation, leave a situation behind that you may not be able to rectify in time to survive. The corporate baby is not able to survive unforeseen accidents as well as the corporate adult is, and an indecisive person in a position of authority is an accident that is walking around waiting to happen. It's only a question of time.

12

Dealing with Mistakes

As you rise in authority and position, you will probably move further and further away from where the action is, and thus become more dependent on reports from subordinate managers to inform you of what is occurring. In addition to acquiring more responsibility as you ascend the management ladder, you tend to deal more and more in the future, to be more concerned with long-range planning, new products or ideas, return on investments, and so on. You can't know in advance whether your long-term plans will work out or not. Only time will tell. The higher up you go, the less you'll know, personally, about the details of the subject you have to make a decision on. The task becomes so large and the time to decide is so short that, many times, the decision has to be made before all factors are known. In some cases, there is no way to know for sure all you would like to know to improve the chance for success.

The entrepreneur is much like the reporter or political analyst who must predict the winner of an election when only 5 to 10 percent of the votes are in. He would like to wait until later on, when

50 percent or more of the returns are in, but he must make the prediction early. In such cases, some people won't make a prediction or decision; they'll wait for further data. The fear of being wrong is so overpowering that when it is time to decide or act, they are immobilized.

There is a tendency for us to rely too much on the opinions of subordinate managers or consultants. If you are uncertain which way to go and your advisers appear confident, there is a strong tendency to follow their advice, even against your own better judgment. Always request and receive as many divergent inputs as possible, and give them due consideration. However, I strongly suggest that you never permit any decision to be made or any action to be taken unless you fully agree with the plan or idea.

In other words, make your own decision. Don't let anyone else do it for you. If it works out well, the advisers will be the first in line to let you and others know it was really their idea and you merely went along with it. If, on the other hand, the decision they recommended was wrong, they will point out that it was your decision, and they merely provided you with information or data.

As a new entrepreneur, you will feel uncertain about and uncomfortable with your new responsibilities. As you mature in your new role and as you realize that you must deal with uncertainty and problems, you will steadily gain more confidence and become more decisive, and will be less afraid of taking risks. Early on, I let some very forceful and confident subordinates and consultants convince me, against my own feelings on the subjects, to make some business and investment decisions. In every case, a disaster followed and I was the loser. In looking back, I realize that my own self-doubts and uncertainty caused me to accept recommendations from others. My advisers acted as if they were sure of themselves, but they were just as uncertain as I was.

Call it intuition, "gut feeling," or whatever, a manager eventually develops a feel for his job. When your inner voice speaks to you, listen to it. It is not just emotion, it is your whole background, training, and experience speaking to you all at once. A doubt enters your mind or you don't like some idea or presentation, but you can't put your feelings into words; all you have is an impression. Even if you are unable to explain why you feel as you do, act on your impressions.

As described in Chapter 8, a large conglomerate expressed an interest in acquiring our company. I declined the offer, and several years later, the big company went bankrupt. If we had gone along, we would have lost everything. There was no "scientific" reason why I said no to them—rather there was an accumulation of impressions I received at various stages of the negotiations. Restriction of sale of the stock meant we would be tied to this new company, win or lose, and we could not exercise our own business judgment on what to do with "our" stock. The opulent office that the president retained indicated to me less concern with costs and profit and more concern with ego gratification and comfort. Finally, the high-pressure presentation turned me off completely. Fancy color slides showing estimates of future growth and earnings have to be based on more than the beauty and expense of the presentation itself. It was all form and no substance.

Many times a management decision has to be made based on little more than how one "feels" about it. Don't be afraid to act on a "feeling," even though it is unscientific. It may be all you have to go with. It is your decision; don't let anyone else make it for you. There is little that can be said in favor of making mistakes except that you can learn from them. If you make your own decision and are wrong, you can at least learn something from the experience. If you let others do it for you, you'll usually lose the most.

Some years ago, at a former place of employment, our general manager addressed the department managers, of which I was a junior member. He said he realized that when we approached him with new ideas or techniques, many times he did not go along with us. He said we should not construe this to mean that he was negative or unresponsive to new ideas, and he asked us to continue to approach him any time we thought we could improve or add new techniques to his division. He said experience had taught him to never agree to anything unless he totally approved of the idea. He was willing to take risks, but he had to believe in and accept the risk or he said no. At the time, I thought that he was being far too conservative. Now, I understand what he meant. As the leader, don't go along with anything you don't understand, because it will generally work to your disadvantage.

For those in middle-level positions, I am not advocating that you refuse to cooperate or that you ignore directives with which you disagree. No one can agree with everything. On the contrary, it is up to you to clearly point out to supervisors how you feel and why. Be sure to specify exactly why you disagree in time for your supervisor to consider your input. If he decides against you, and it is his right to do so, it is up to you to go along with it or do your best.

However, if it is a serious matter that concerns a moral issue or an action you believe can adversely affect your career, you will have to take a stand and pay the consequences. This is no easy thing to do, but going along with something that you have very strong feelings against can have serious effects on you later. This is a question of judgment, and only time will tell. Do it your way if you are in charge. As an old friend of mine says, "Brush your own teeth and make your own decisions." If others decide for you regularly, and if they make the right decisions, then they should have your job. If they are wrong, you probably will eventually lose out. If you are boss, make your own decisions and be judged by the results.

In doing it your way, you will make mistakes. We all make mistakes. "The person who never makes mistakes, never makes anything." Most of us pay the price for the mistakes we make, or the mistakes others make in our behalf. When we do something correctly, we don't learn anything, because we knew just what to do, and we did it well. To benefit from mistakes we have to view them in their proper perspective. Just as those who do not study history are doomed to repeat it.

If a mistake occurs at work, don't try to hide it or lie about it. The effects of that type of behavior are generally far worse than the mistake itself, and do severe and permanent damage to all concerned. I would rather be known as someone who makes a few honest mistakes than as someone whose word could not be relied upon. We all make mistakes. How we handle them is what matters. Some people try to avoid mistakes by avoiding decisions. They don't understand that by doing nothing they are making the biggest mistake of all. Bud Wilkinson, the famous football coach, described football as "a game in which 50,000 people who need exercise sit and watch 22 boys who need rest." You won't make mistakes if you don't play, but you won't score goals either.

Let us discuss those who do things and therefore make their share of mistakes. How do they handle their mistakes? What do they do about them? How do they go on when they know they will make more mistakes? Some people try to hide or suppress an error. If anyone suspects, they deny, obfuscate, argue, cry, fight, or go home—but they do not admit to any mistakes. It hurts too much. This person arrived at level one of the "error correction process," but would not permit himself to go on. If he doesn't admit to making a mistake, he will never benefit from the costly lessons that errors can teach us. He paid the tuition but he stopped going to class. The same mistake will happen over and over again, because he didn't admit to himself that there was ever anything to correct in the first place. Little can be done with such people. They won't let anyone help them.

Let us proceed to level two of our error correction process. Once you realize you have made a mistake and accept that fact, what are you going to do about it? Your mental processes and outlook on life take over. Are you willing to discuss it openly with others without getting your ego bent out of shape? Can you accept comments or criticism about your mistake from others? If so, you are doing well. If not, you're stalled at level two of the error correction process.

Level three is the learning stage. Here is where you can benefit from your mistake. (I would estimate that by this stage we have left behind 75 to 80 percent of error makers. They are unwilling or unable to pass through levels one and two.) By freely discussing your mistake and asking for help, you can receive information and assistance from others. Ask for and seek information and discuss what has occurred, so you can see what you should or should not do next time. Don't fake it, because even if you do fool everyone else, which is unlikely, you can't deceive yourself, and it is what you think about yourself that matters most. Lies and deceit are temporary shelters and they tend to destroy those who choose to live there.

Some managers appreciate being advised by subordinates when an error has occurred. Are you one of these? Other managers are understanding when a subordinate tells them about a mistake, but when they discover it for themselves of when some superior or customer lays it on them, that is another story. If you don't let subordinates discuss your errors and if you react negatively to criticism from below, you won't get any comments except agreement. You won't go far in that job or under those circumstances, because you won't receive your subordinates' true opinions or comments. They will be afraid of you.

The trick is not to be a repeater. Don't make the same mistake twice. Be creative—always make new mistakes, so you can learn new things. Unfortunately, most people are repeaters. They make the same mistake over and over again and bury their careers. Those of us who go to confession could tape a visit and it would probably apply each week; we'd find the same mistakes and the same misdeeds recurring in the same order and magnitude. So you see, some of us do tend to be repeaters in the mistakes we all make.

Every office has its share of chronic latecomers. Tardiness is a bad habit that some people simply do not choose to change. There are the "doers" and the "watchers." People with poor work habits who are too set in their ways to change are hung up on level one of the error correction process. They can't be helped, because they won't be helped. There are some people who will quickly and surely refuse help when offered, but will gladly discuss your past and present errors and mistakes with you or anyone else. (I think this type of person keeps a file on everyone else.) There are chronic complainers and critics. These people are hung up on level two of our process. They too are difficult to help. Although they know they make mistakes, they won't let anyone discuss it, so they become repeaters.

In the "level-three group" we find some very successful people. They seem to rise up through the ranks wherever they work. These are the so-called lucky ones, who seem to prosper in spite of all the mistakes they made in their careers. The old saying, "Fool me once, shame on you; fool me twice, shame on me," is accepted, understood, and applied by these people. They make many mistakes, but you don't find them repeating the same mistakes very often if at all. They learn and grow.

A frank and open admission that you have made a mistake and an explanation of how you plan to correct it is usually very well received by all concerned. In hiding, suppressing, or avoiding the issue, you reveal to superiors and subordinates that mistakes cannot be easily discussed with you. As an entrepreneur, you want to always be made aware of any mistake that can affect your small venture. The climate and environment that you foster can either encourage an open discussion of mistakes or can keep them hidden and suppressed until they suddenly smash down on you from all sides and without warning. The choice is yours.

The lesson to be learned is this: The more things we do, the more mistakes we will make. That is as certain as tomorrow's sunrise. It is what we do after we make a mistake that counts.

But don't let fear of making a mistake prevent you from doing your job. In the small business venture you are the decision maker, and that is how it should be. Listen to as many sources of information or advice as you can, then do it your way. Sometimes you will be right and sometimes you will be wrong. It is your batting average that counts. In delegating authority and responsibility to others, you are deciding which subjects to retain for yourself and which subjects to allow others to choose courses of action for. This is not a cop out. It's part of doing it your way, and it is up to you to use your own good judgment on how and when you do it. If you are not afraid to make a mistake now and then, and if you are able to understand and learn from mistakes, then do it your way and win or lose by your own decisions and good judgment. Play the game you want, and the way you believe it should be played. You will be playing for real, not for fun, so don't let anyone ever convince you to follow any course of action that you don't agree with at the time. Employees or consultants can and will make mistakes. They get paid while they do it, and you pay the price. If your venture fails, they'll find work elsewhere; you'll be left with the corporate body to bury.

Delegate authority, but don't give up too much or permit subordinates or consultants to "gobbledygook" you into letting them do anything that you don't agree with. You don't have to know how they do it, but you have to know what they are doing, why, and how much it will cost. These are your main areas of concern. Do it your way and don't let others do it their way unless you agree with them.

If you discuss the subject of making decisions and making mistakes with other entrepreneurs or senior managers, you'll probably find lots of people who went through this difficult process and learned the lessons the hard way. In fact, this area caused me much trouble and came close to smashing our new venture during the first five years. My uncertainty in sailing in new and uncharted waters caused me to vacillate and to accept judgments and opinions from others. In looking back (hindsight is a cruel messenger), I can now see what I did and why. Once again, it is your ship, your decisions of where to go, when, why, and how. *Do it your way.* You lose the most if you are wrong and *you* gain the most if you are right.

13

Disagreements, Discipline, and Dismissals

As with anything else in life, everything involved in running a small business isn't all beer and skittles. There are unpleasant aspects as well as pleasant ones. The concept of the small team working joyously and harmoniously together against the outside competition is all well and good, but people are people wherever they work and whatever they do. Problems do come up. As previously discussed, internal bickering at the highest level in small ventures has destroyed a number of good, growing outfits. Problems at the lower levels, too, can cause serious trouble, because each person in a small business is more important than in an organization of thousands, wherein the individual effort, except under very unusual circumstances, is lost or not recognized at the higher levels. The friendly informality of the small venture can cause serious problems when disagreements arise or when discipline or dismissal is necessary. You are all very likely working in proximity to each other, and everyone is probably on a first-name basis, so it is wise to have formal procedures to handle the unpleasant but necessary aspects of running a business. Never make a decision or take action while you're angry or upset; you'll probably regret it. This is a time for cool, dispassionate deliberation and judgment. You don't want a lawsuit on your hands at any time, much less during the first few years of your corporate life, so let's discuss some procedures for you to consider and possibly use to your advantage.

Disagreements

The word disagreement carries an unpleasant connotation, that of dissension, argument, or difficulty. However, much good can come from disagreement, if you disagree properly and avoid the unfortunate negative side effects that accompany it. You must encourage people to express their points of view, even dissenting ones, so you can benefit from their opinions. Everyone enjoys approval and applause. Being human, and our egos being what they are, most of us seek out those who agree with us and avoid those who do not. However, in a business or working environment, this is not always possible. In fact, it is not even desirable to look for and associate with only those who do things your way or who always agree with you. It may be comfortable and pleasant, but is it productive?

I suggest that you seek out, encourage, and foster disagreement, but be sure to handle it properly. Do not allow the situation to degenerate into opposing camps harboring hostility and distrust. In a small business, the person in charge must be able to encourage people to express their ideas and plans by creating an environment that does not suppress a free exchange of ideas. However, he must not go too far, or people will "talk things to death" and never come to any meaningful decisions or conclusions.

There are some techniques and tools that can be used advantageously when you apply your own judgment in handling disagreement or criticism. But before we get into techniques, let's briefly discuss the types of people with whom we work or are associated.

1. *The know-it-all.* This fellow can and does tell everyone what he thinks. He comes on loud and clear. He is rarely there when a decision has to be made, but afterward he is Johnny-on-the-spot telling you what was wrong. And he is never wrong—if you don't believe me, just ask him.

2. *The shy person.* This person is so quiet you would never know he is around unless you hear him breathing. He does the work assigned to him. He rarely, if ever, ventures an opinion or disagrees with anyone. He doesn't want to hurt anyone's feelings, and even if he is sure something is going to go wrong, he doesn't say anything. He just lets it happen. He would never presume to suggest to the boss or to anyone else that there is a better way to do anything. This could cause controversy, and the shrinking violet doesn't like to be the subject of controversy.

3. *The I-only-follow-orders type.* This person does what he is told and doesn't ask questions. Whether or not his activities have any value is not for him to say. He may disagree or give his ideas when asked, but unless he is specifically requested to do so he'll remain silent and never question anything.

4. *The type who opposes for the sake of opposing.* This type likes to argue and disagree. No matter what you plan to do or what decision you want to make, you can count on him to disagree. He seems to feel that the only way he can show you he has a mind of his own is to disagree with just about everything and everyone. I have been told this is a form of arrested emotional development in which a person's intellect and body continue to grow, but he stopped developing emotionally at the age of 13. Most of us know a few people like this. Unpleasant, aren't they?

5. *The sensible person.* This type of person is willing and able to offer fresh ideas and is not afraid to disagree with someone else or to suggest an alternative plan. However, he must be given the right environment in which to respond. Fortunately, the majority of

people fall into this category. Management should develop a climate in which they are encouraged to express disagreement or to propose new and better ways to do things.

On occasion, those in categories 1, 2, 3 and 4 do come up with some good ideas (even a broken clock is correct twice a day). Fortunately, people in those categories are rare enough to be handled on an individual basis. So set up your system to take care of the sensible people in your organization and deal with the others on an individual basis. Don't let types 1 through 4 interfere with or upset your system to encourage and receive comments or disagreement from the majority.

You are the manager and you are responsible for the outfit. You have to assign work to other people and monitor their progress through one or several layers of intermediate managers. You have to make decisions, many times based upon information others bring to you. You are responsible for the organization's efforts. You should want people to come to you with their ideas and to disagree with you if they think something is wrong or could be done better. Your employees won't agree with everything you do, but you don't want them to be silent and to blindly go along with all of your decisions.

Somewhere between hostile rebellion and blind acquiescence lies the healthy, productive exchange of ideas. How you get your company there depends on your personality and judgment, the procedure you set up, and the way you conduct yourself.

Suggestion boxes are good for morale, but generally little of real or lasting value comes out of them. Issues such as the number of parking spaces, the placement of coffee machines, and the quality of cafeteria food are most often raised. We did get one good suggestion. An employee put a note in the suggestion box and said that he and others had been bumping into the suggestion boxes in the halls. He said they were a safety hazard and suggested that we remove them. We removed the boxes and gave him an award for a beneficial suggestion.

There are times when a change or directive *must* be implemented. A new IRS regulation, a change in Social Security deductions, a new or revised law, safety regulations, or a client's preference leave an employer no choice. In such cases, disagreement or argument among staff is counterproductive and merely compounds any problems associated with the implementation of such changes or rules. Any change, improvement, or deviation is beyond the control of the company. It is up to management, in such cases, to clearly define and explain what is about to happen and why. Also, it should be clearly explained there are no exceptions, and none will be permitted. Get it done and over with as soon as possible. Added discussions accomplish nothing.

Here are techniques that help encourage those at the lower end of the chain of command to disagree with procedures and to try to change things, and some things to keep in mind when offering advice to others. Again, use your own good judgment in implementing the methods described below. All of them may not apply in any one business environment; it is up to you to decide where and when they fit and if they should be used.

The boss wants ideas. In this situation the boss has a decision or a plan to make. The higher up the boss is, the less certain he may be about what to do. If there are many variables or unknowns, the wise manager will try to gather as much information as possible about the subject by drawing on current and past experiences. "What happened before? Why? Is it likely to occur again? What, if anything, is different about what I plan to do now?" The boss is about to gamble and he wants to tilt the odds in his favor, so he asks for input from others up and down the line. He encourages employees to freely discuss the topic at hand, making it clear that he has the right to accept or reject the ideas presented. He has to make the decision and he wants to weigh and consider other opinions from people whose judgment is respected. Once the final course of action is chosen, the boss should explain why the decision was made and why some suggestions were not followed.

Unless the decision maker does this, he will find that those whose ideas were not accepted will tend to fall silent; they feel that they are not heard or that their suggestions are not given any serious attention. Critics have a valid role in giving new insight or noting imperfections in any plan or decision. The trick is to get their reaction before, not after, the decision is made, so you'll have time to re-examine the plan before it is put into effect. If you are among those chosen to contribute your ideas, consider it a compliment every time you are asked. If you are the boss who solicits constructive criticism and new ideas, consider yourself fortunate if you are able to regularly receive honest dissenting opinions before you act. You will surely get them afterward, and often from the most unexpected and uninformed sources.

Several years ago we hired a retired Air Force colonel for a senior position on our technical staff. He is excellent and we are fortunate to have him and his expertise with our company. One day he came to me with a suggestion. He said that in the military, the senior person generally had a very direct method of communicating to his senior staff. It was called an executive memo and it was on paper of a specific color, so that everyone knew it was a special communication that got top-priority attention and response. He suggested that I adopt this procedure for communications to the senior managers. This appealed to me for two reasons. First, it was an excellent suggestion; on occasion, my memos to the managers were misplaced. Second, we had a large supply of green paper that was of a shade the secretaries did not like and therefore weren't using. Now, when a high-priority item comes up, I send an executive memo on the green paper, and I get an immediate response. I don't use this method too often, so when I do send a "green memo" it stands out.

Offering unsolicited advice or disagreement. A friend who is a lawyer once told me, "Free advice is worth what you pay for it, which is nothing." Very few people accept unsolicited advice or dissent easily. Before you offer someone the benefit of your opinion, carefully consider the potential effects. You can come out of it a hero or a bum, depending on how the person accepts what you say and whether later events prove you to be right or wrong. You should know the recipient very well, proceed very carefully at each step, and be prepared to stop quickly when you meet resistance.

By presuming upon a friendship or close relationship with a boss or subordinate and giving unsolicited advice, you may jeopardize your career, a personal friendship, or a good working relationship. So be cautious. If you do speak your mind, be sure to do it *before* the action takes place, not after. Negative comments about what has already taken place are deadly and generally unproductive, but if you feel compelled to say something ex post facto, I suggest the following scenario.

Ask the person if you may speak to him about the issue at hand. Carefully explain that you realize your advice or comments were not solicited. Then ask if he would like to hear your comments. Don't go on unless the answer is a very definite "yes." Do not write unsolicited critical memos; say what you have to say in private. Tell no one else, especially if the person accepts your comments and changes the decision or plan. Don't do it too often. The boss will invite you, in the future, if he wants your advice again. Few people *ever* go to a superior on their own to disagree with a plan or procedure. From silence, one assumes general agreement.

Soliciting and offering comments on failures. After a plan has been put into effect, a wise manager will solicit comments on it, especially if it was successful. People are much more likely to give honest advice or disagreement concerning a plan that has worked out than they are about a failure. They are not afraid to speak out about the minor things that go wrong, and since these things can be corrected in the future, those are precisely the things the boss wants to hear about. In the case of a failure, many use "diaper management," in which they try to cover their own tails before they suggest what went wrong or why. As Napoleon said, "Victory has a thousand fathers, but defeat is an orphan."

Offering unsolicited advice concerning an unsuccessful plan or decision is so obviously dangerous that only the most foolhardy or desperate person would ever attempt it. Whenever possible, try to give your opponent an opportunity to "save face." In proving your point or winning your argument, do not pin him down or force him to admit a mistake to you or others in order for corrective action to follow. Being human, most of us bitterly resent attempts to box us in or prove us wrong. We all have egos and will react negatively to disagreement that is based upon criticism of our own performance, decisions, or judgments. There is hardly any benefit that will accrue to you if you win some point by disagreement, but in so doing you offend someone else. You gain an enemy at work and that is not a good idea. And others who watch you operate will certainly remember. At work, we need all of the help and all of the friends we can get. During a disagreement be careful not to hurt any feelings or damage any egos. Egos are very fragile and take a very long time to mend, if they mend at all.

Disagreement and dissent can be beneficial or disruptive depending upon how the manager copes with it and how the individuals concerned react to it. It is a touchy subject that requires special effort and maturity by both the giver and receiver. It can be judged only by evaluating the long-term effects. If it works for you, use it; if not, don't. There are no hard-and-fast rules to follow, but the techniques described above have been used with some success in the past.

Keep in mind that I am not discussing disagreement over moral or ethical issues. I am talking about pragmatic day-to-day decisions of a business nature. Personally held beliefs on moral or ethical questions are a matter of conscience and should never be compromised. In fact, when a moral issue is involved, you may disregard all of the above. Techniques matter little in such serious situations. To be honest with yourself, you should go directly to the person with whom you disagree on a moral issue and point of ethics, tell him why, and then make a decision about how to proceed. Should you leave or can you change what offends you? This is a decision only you can make.

Discipline

When you have to handle a serious problem, internal company discipline should be a formal procedure. The disciplinary interview (D.I.) should be called after a series of minor offenses have had a substantial cumulative effect or when someone has committed a major offense from which dismissal could result. You should not need to call a large number of such interviews. A D.I. is disturbing to everyone concerned, and even if you win your case you may acquire a reputation as someone who cannot handle his people or as someone who is too strict or severe in your supervision of others. In either situation, you come up the loser. The teacher who sends too many pupils to the principal's office for discipline will eventually be called in to explain why. Before you call for a formal D.I., try to informally solve the problem by having a quiet chat, by giving some encouragement, or by transferring or reassigning the person involved. In many situations, the problem can be worked out to mutual advantage without recourse to a formal D.I.

You may have concluded that I am avoiding or trying to postpone the formal D.I. I am, because experience indicates that most formal disciplinary interviews don't solve the real problem. Each person tries to defend his position, and the battle lines become so drawn and fixed that there is very little opportunity for give and take. Under those circumstances, there are no winners, only losers, and one side loses more than the other. If interviews are such a problem for all concerned and there is little chance to really solve the problem or restore the situation, then, as the fellow said when told not to look up at the solar eclipse with the naked eye, "If they are so dangerous, why do we have them?"

o A formal D.I. procedure is good for employee morale (even if the person involved eventually leaves, as most do), because those remaining know they will not be disciplined or dismissed in a casual way or in a burst of anger. They know that they have a right to be heard.

○ A formal D.I. could reveal to higher management that the problems rest with the manager, not with the defendant.

○ If your growing organization hires union employees, a D.I. will probably be required.

○ The D.I. reduces the possibility of a lawsuit later, from an unhappy former employee who claims his legal rights were violated or that he was improperly dismissed without just cause.

If you find that a disciplinary interview is required, then you as the boss had better do your homework, in advance. I suggest you do the following:

1. See the immediate supervisor of the person involved. Explain that the person has been acting up again and that you think a formal D.I. is necessary now, and that a dismissal notice may be in order if the undesirable behavior doesn't stop. Prior to this stage, several attempts should have been made to talk to and reason with the person. Let us assume that all agree that the D.I. is in order.

2. Follow the company's policies and procedures on the D.I. to the letter. The policies should require that you notify the concerned party some days prior to the interview to give him time to prepare his defense. (He may also prepare an offensive against you, so consider this as a real possibility and prepare yourself.)

3. Prepare the case in writing. Put down every detail you can think of that has contributed to the situation. Your daily log will be invaluable in this situation. Your case is stronger if you are able to state that other people have experienced the same or similar problems with the person.

4. Do not in any way give the impression that you are acting out of spite, anger, or resentment. Let the person know that you are acting in the best interests of the organization. You, as the boss, have a problem with an individual and, with regret, you have de-

cided that it is so bad that a formal D.I. must be called to settle the matter once and for all.

5. Show that although you have tried a number of times to solve the problem informally by warning the person, he has not responded. You must show that you have clearly tried to explain how serious the situation is to the person concerned. You can be sure that he will deny the allegations or will try to convince you that previous warnings never took place. Or he may indicate that he thought you weren't really serious or that you didn't make yourself clear. You can see the value of writing a memo to the person concerned prior to initiating formal interview procedures, and of receiving a written response. If you have copies of such correspondence, no one can deny your previous attempts to solve the problem informally.

6. You may request that other management personnel attend, but don't force anyone to. That could create greater resentment against you later on. Let us assume now that the interview is scheduled and, naturally, you, as the boss, have to attend. What will happen there? What should you say? Some of the following things will come up for discussion.

○ The defendant may claim that personal prejudice led to the interview. He may claim that someone is jealous or is out to get him. Even religious or race prejudice may be claimed in the defense.

○ He may claim that you are not a good manager and that you caused most of the problem yourself. He will have his own facts and figures to present.

○ The burden of proof lies with you, and you will probably speak first, so make it good. Give a detailed account and try to present your position before the defendant gets his turn at bat.

○ Present your case quietly, forcefully, and quickly, and try to work from written material as much as possible. Verbal dueling at this stage is fruitless; so are anger and accusations.

○ You will be expected to state what discipline is in order: sus-
pension, fine, transfer, demotion, or dismissal. Propose only
one that you have carefully thought out in advance, and
don't discuss or present alternatives. It will weaken the case.

○ Stand by to defend yourself against a counterattack.

There's no denying that a disciplinary interview is a bad experience for everyone. Even if the employee "shapes up" and returns
to his former position in your organization, things will never be the
same. There may be a recurrence or open resentment from him.
Generally, formal interviews eventually result in departures—the
person may resign, be transferred, or be dismissed. Other employees may resign in protest. If you act in favor of the employee re-
quiring discipline, his manager may resent it and leave.

At best, the D.I. shows all employees that they have certain
rights that the company or organization will observe. But it should
be avoided if at all possible. Even if a marriage counselor convinces
a man and a woman who no longer love each other to stay together, their marriage will never be the same. Something has gone
that will never return. It then becomes a business relationship and
any marriage should be much more than that. If you and someone
else have to attend a formal disciplinary interview in order to work
together, something is missing from your relationship. If you, as the
boss, find yourself conducting numerous such interviews, then look
within yourself.

At former places of employment, I have participated in two disciplinary interviews, as a member of the management committee
that heard the interview and had to make the final decision. They
were both unpleasant; I hope that you never see or hear one up
close, but it may be necessary now and then.

Dismissal

One of the most disagreeable tasks that any entrepreneur, manager, or boss has to face is the dismissal of a subordinate. If you

remove someone from the corporate body for good and sufficient reasons, and for the good of the company, you are cutting off a limb to save the body. It hurts everyone involved, so do it carefully and as humanely as possible. It is so unpleasant that many bosses and supervisors avoid doing it, at the peril of their own operation; or they make mistakes when they do it.

Let's assume that someone has to be terminated. It is up to you, as the boss, to take action. If you don't, a much worse situation will develop. It is assumed that the person to be terminated has been given a number of warnings and a formal disciplinary interview. (This is a safe assumption, because most managers and supervisors tend to let a bad situation go on too long before they finally act.) When you do act, do it cooly, calmly, carefully, legally, and strictly by the book.

Never, absolutely never, fire anyone while you are angry. A man was caught stealing gallons of paint from the factory where he worked. His boss was so angry that he forgot about the union grievance procedure and the company's formal dismissal procedure, and fired the thief on the spot. The union filed a complaint against the company, and the man was reinstated to his job. If the boss had followed proper procedure, the union very likely would have agreed to a dismissal.

Never dismiss anyone publicly. Being fired is bad enough for someone without the added humiliation of having it done in front of co-workers or even strangers. If you dismiss someone that way, stand by for a lawsuit.

Don't be informal when dismissing anyone. A quiet verbal dismissal that results in the quick departure of the offending employee may be followed by a claim for unemployment compensation. Unemployment adjusters require written evidence upon which to make their decisions. It's up to you to provide it. Employers (the companies) pay 100 percent of the costs of federal and state unemployment insurance. No taxes or contributions from the employees are involved. However, most employees believe that they contribute to unemployment insurance (many confuse it with Social Security taxes) and they don't hesitate to run down to the local unemployment office to file a claim. If you state that an employee was dismissed for good cause, you had better have written records to prove it. You can be sure the applicant won't tell the real reason. If he does, he won't get the checks. Your company's contribution to unemployment insurance is computed on the basis of claims paid to former employees and your company has to restore to the fund payments made to former employees. It definitely will work to your disadvantage if you dismiss someone verbally, and later on he collects unemployment checks. You wouldn't like to have your contributions to this account increased because you didn't keep records of reasons for a dismissal, would you?

If you become angry or upset during an informal, verbal dismissal and say the wrong thing or inadvertently refer to the person's sex, age, race, or religion in a derogatory way, you are in for trouble. That's against the law, and no matter how valid the reasons for the dismissal may have been, a whole new affair may open up and you won't like it. So don't be informal in a dismissal.

Don't talk about a dismissal to any unauthorized people. After you have dismissed someone, it is natural for other employees or clients to ask you where the person is. If you say that someone was fired and give the reasons, then again stand by for a possible lawsuit. If the terminated employee can prove that your remarks in any way hurt him or hindered his chances for finding another job, the roof may fall in on you personally and on the company you represent as well. The fact that what you said was true is irrelevant. You may later have to prove it in a court of law, and that's an entirely different ball game. Even if you win the lawsuit, you haven't done anything but defend yourself, and who needs the aggravation? Going to court as the defendant is not a profitable expenditure of time and effort. Also, you won't like the publicity at all. This sort of thing definitely won't help your company.

Never give someone you've dismissed a bad reference. "If you can't say anything good about him, then say nothing." Giving a bad reference can result in lawsuits, because the next company may advise the applicant why he wasn't offered a position and may tell him exactly what you said. This happens even when the other company assures you that all your comments will be held strictly in confidence. With the new right-to-know laws now in existence, it is difficult for even a lawyer to know exactly what and what not to do and say. So, it's best not to say anything bad about any current or former employee, especially if you own the company or a substantial part of it.

Don't give false references. After the offending person leaves and things on the job improve and passions cool down, it is natural for you to feel regret, sorrow, and even some compassion for the former employee. We all tend to cool off with time. Suppose you receive a request for a reference weeks, months, or even years later. (I received calls for references on former employees who had left ten years before.) You may feel that the real story of the person's dismissal will damage him, but that no response might hurt him too, so you try to be a nice guy and give a good—but false—reference. Who knows, in a new environment, with a new boss, the person may work out fine. He can't hurt you, so why be mean?

Here's an example of what can happen in such situations. A person was fired for theft. The reason for dismissal was put on his personnel record and filed away. Later, a request for a reference came in. The former boss, in trying to be a nice guy, wrote and forwarded a good recommendation to the new employer. The applicant was hired, and guess what? He stole from his new employer. He escaped with a large amount of cash and valuables. The police became involved and, in checking out the background of this person, his employment record and reason for dismissal from his former position became known. It was clear that his old boss sent in a false recommendation. A lawsuit followed in which the person's former company was sued and had to pay damages. All of this is frightening, especially to you, as the boss.

To avoid problems, consider implementing the following procedures:

1. Prior to the dismissal, prepare a written document for your company records and state the reasons for your decision that the person be dismissed. If you can, include substantiating reports from junior managers.
2. Discuss your decision with your managers in private, and get the appropriate manager's concurrence in writing. Keep a copy in the files.
3. Agree on the date of dismissal with the person's manager.
4. On the agreed-upon date, have the person involved come to your office after working hours. Your company lawyer, personnel manager, or some other third party should be present to witness the affair. When you dismiss the employee, tell him why, pay him for a reasonable termination period, and escort him out. Have those who were present each write and send to you a formal memo about the dismissal indicating their concurrence with the action. File these memos.
5. Show no anger and don't argue. Keep it cool and businesslike.
6. If you have a personnel officer, you may be able to let personnel handle it all. In that case, turn it over to that department and stay out of it. Your company rules, however, may require your presence.
7. Tell no one about it, not even family members. They may repeat it at the store or elsewhere, and you never know who is within earshot.
8. If people at work ask about the person who's been fired, just say he left and let it go at that. Say nothing more.

As difficult as it is to dismiss someone, he generally knows it is coming and most of the worry about a big fight is needless. The arguing period is over now, and most said they expected it. Most dismissals in which I have been involved were caused by problems of attitude, in which the person refused to cooperate with other employees or with his manager. I have never had to fire anyone for stealing or for violence, and I hope I never do. However, I have been advised that, even in these situations the person being fired was quiet and repentant when dismissed.

In dismissing someone, the form in which it is done is just as important as the reason for which it is done. All in all, it is a very unpleasant part of any boss's job. When it's necessary, it must be done quietly, efficiently, and legally, so you can return to normal operations quickly and forget all about it. The ramifications of a dismissal handled incorrectly are so great and potentially damaging that it is well worth your time and trouble to get competent legal advice in advance. It may be that you can get into trouble before you know what you are doing and pay the price later. When our passions are aroused and we are angry and upset, we tend to say or do stupid things that we later regret. As your company grows, it is only a question of time before you will have to handle a formal dismissal, so it's best to establish the procedures and think about it now. Whatever your company's policies are, follow them to the letter. You can be careless and slipshod in how you promote or give raises. Form doesn't matter here, it is the substance that counts. But in dismissals, forms, policies, and legal procedures are paramount and mandatory.

A final word on this subject. One way I have found to avoid this whole unpleasant affair is to advise the person to quietly resign and depart. In over 99 percent of these situations, the person involved sees the value of a quiet resignation and will be only too happy to leave that way. Most will want to work elsewhere, and they realize that a formal dismissal, for cause, won't do them or their careers any good. This course is preferable to disciplinary interviews, formal hearings, and dismissals. However, there are some situations in which far more than just a dismissal may be involved (such as theft, violence, or damage to company property), so it's best to prepare, with strong legal advice, your company's formal grievance, disciplinary, and dismissal procedures. They're like fire extinguishers; you hope you'll never need them, but if you use them only once, then it was well worth the trouble to have them ready. Everyone feels safer just knowing they are there.

14

When and How to Leave

There are few things as unpleasant as a guest who overstays his welcome. But when a founding entrepreneur stays on too long in charge of his operation, lots of people can be hurt. You're going to have to turn over the reins to someone who is better qualified to continue the operation than you are. Since there are many different types of companies, the point in time when this should occur will vary, but there are some situations that indicate that the time has come.

1. When the company becomes too large for one person to handle in an informal way, it is big enough for a bureaucracy to take over. Since most entrepreneurs don't operate well in a bureaucracy, they tend to interfere and meddle in the various levels or spheres of authority and mess up the works. They still roam the factory or office and talk to everyone the way they did in the old days, only it's not the old days anymore. No one dares to suggest that they step down, but that's exactly what they should do.

2. The entrepreneur is not trained to handle high finance, plant

expansion problems, tax problems, union negotiations, and so on. Someone with an MBA degree and 10 years' experience may now be much better qualified to run the show.

3. New techniques, ideas, procedures may be called for, and the entrepreneur may not be as responsive or receptive to any changes as he once was. He brought up this baby, so why change things now, when it's doing so well?

Napoleon was reputed to have said that most generals are always busy preparing for the last war. Those who experienced action as junior officers move to higher levels of authority 20 or 30 years later, so it is not difficult to understand why the new war finds generals using ancient and outdated tactics and strategy. The founding entrepreneur, like the general, may want to use the same business tactics and strategies that worked so well 10 or 20 years ago when the business was small and those procedures were correct for that point in time. Now, however, with a larger, more diverse organization, the same methods or techniques may be all wrong. Try telling that to a grizzled, old, successful entrepreneur. Very few of them could stand it, and you might be shown the door while you're in mid-sentence.

4. Serendipity may come into play and your company may stumble upon or be offered an opportunity in an entirely new business area that is unrelated to the entrepreneur's field of interest or capability. Either he may not recognize the opportunity (or risk) or he may say, "It's not our line of work," and let the opportunity pass.

This has happened to our company. Recently we were offered an opportunity for new business in an area related to computer software that we have no expertise in. We are trying to cope with and respond to it now, and it is very difficult. Better advance planning on my part could have helped anticipate this opportunity in time for us to prepare for it. This sort of thing occurs sooner or later in every small venture. In most cases, the reason for failure to capitalize on those opportunities rests with the entrepreneur, who is only interested in his one special area of expertise.

5. When it's time for breaking down the responsibility into several distinct cost centers, authority *must* be given to other people. There is too much going on for one person to understand well enough to make timely decisions.

As the enterprise prospers, the whole corporate structure should be changed. Yet the "old boy" won't let go. Now the problems start, and they can be serious. Within the organization, either formally or informally, a "work around the boss" system starts to develop. This sort of thing has happened very often, yet each entrepreneur somehow feels that he is different, and it won't happen to him. It's only a question of time, in most cases. As stated earlier, entrepreneurs generally don't get as much out of their operations as those who follow up and take over when they leave. You, as the entrepreneur, had better accept this fact of business life. Plan for and cooperate with your replacement and you will be well taken care of. You can arrange for a nice soft spot on the board at your former salary with all sorts of perks, and no one will care whether you show up for meetings or not. Most people will probably prefer that you don't show up. They don't want to hear any more "war stories" of how tough it was 10 or 20 years ago, and how you repeatedly saved the company from disaster. They want to treat you with the courtesy, respect, and consideration you deserve, but they have jobs to do. If you fight them, then everyone loses. You lose, they lose, and the corporation loses—but you can lose the most. You don't want to be forced out kicking and screaming, do you? That has happened many times. Here are a few cases in which the entrepreneur left under less-than-ideal circumstances.

An entrepreneur left a big company because of a dispute over the type of new products to manufacture, and started his own venture with 20 engineers. He succeeded brilliantly. In less than ten years, the company had sales of more than $150 million annually. However, he was not able to handle such a large operation. The company got into tax problems and had to borrow money to get going again. The creditors wanted a new corporate president, one who was more business oriented. The entrepreneur fought back, but was voted out by his own board. The entrepreneur dragged the fight through the newspapers and into the courts. Who is right? Who is wrong? Who cares? The whole messy affair damages the corporation, no matter who "wins." If the majority of the board thinks it's time for you to step down, then give it some serious thought. No one is indispensable.

In another case, a tailor opened up a clothing store. As his business flourished, he opened up branch stores. His two sons came into the business after they graduated from college. The father knew a lot about clothes but not too much about business, and he failed to adjust his business as time went by. His sons tried to modernize the stores and wanted to shut down branches that were losing money, including the father's first store. The old man reacted violently, and in the ensuing battle, all the stores closed. Everyone was a loser.

A business article about merger and acquisition opportunities identified conditions to look for if you want to acquire a small company at bargain rates. The article stated that (1) when the leader becomes ill or gets old and (2) when the leader dies suddenly, you are likely to get a bargain. An ailing entrepreneur or his surviving family will accept a lower price for the company than it is really worth.

Be aware that many people engage in such practices. Although you or I couldn't take advantage of someone else's misfortune, others see nothing wrong it in at all. It isn't illegal. Some people aren't nice. If you don't plan to protect your interest after you go, no one else will. Plan now, while you have time, the power, and the authority to leave things the way that is best for you and your family.

When the president of a company was murdered in his motel room, the company was thrown into complete chaos. The president had been the only person with authority to sign checks. No employees or suppliers were paid for several months. Many employees left, because they weren't getting any paychecks. This episode rocked the small company to its foundation. Fortunately, it survived and eventually prospered, but it was touch-and-go for about six months and could have easily swung the other way. Lack of planning by the corporate officers nearly made the president's demise and the company's demise one and the same event.

There is no question that a company's founding father serves a very important role in starting the corporate infant, in giving it life, and seeing it through the tough early years. Human parents give life to, raise, and sacrifice everything for the children. But you can't plan your children's lives. You want a doctor and your son becomes a shepherd in Montana. You want a lawyer and your daughter becomes a professional disco dancer. You can't do anything about it now. You had 20 years or so to instill in your child the ideas, morals, and attitudes that you felt were proper. Now you have to let go and see what your handiwork is going to turn out to be.

It's exactly the same with a company. There is a time when you have to let go, so plan for it. If you can select the person you want to replace you, then do so, and spend a few years grooming him. When he takes over, let him do things his way. You have a right to give your opinion and advice, but you aren't in charge any more, so don't try to stay on too long. When it's time to say goodbye, say goodbye and go.

If the founder stays around after he steps down, some senior staff may not accept the new president as the one with the full authority. Some managers may continue to look to the founder to approve the new president's directives. Even though this may do wonders for your ego, it is bad for business. Don't hang around after you leave the top spot. (If you are on the board you can stay there.) If former subordinates call you for a talk, refer them to the new president. It's only fair.

Most large and successful organizations have rules regarding when top people must step down. The military and police organizations have very strict regulations in this regard. Exceptions have been made in very unusual and unique situations, for General MacArthur, for example, but these are very special cases. How many MacArthurs come along in a lifetime? You may like to think that you are one, in your organization, but the odds are that you aren't. If you really are that unique and valuable to your organization, others will tell you and you won't have to say so yourself.

As the top person in your organization, you will have to set up retirement policies. You can't force others to leave, but exempt yourself from your own regulations. Establish either a point in time, a specific age, a corporate size, gross sales, profits, or whatever for your planned departure. Discuss it openly with your principals and your board. When the time comes to leave, then leave.

Pass the baton on to the next runner in the corporate race and let him take off. Your part of the race is over. You have done well. Can you imagine a relay race in which the second runner reaches back for the baton and the first runner won't give it up? You can be sure he won't win the race. The other runners are too fresh and strong. No matter how good you are, if you run the whole race while your competitors use fresh runners every quarter mile or so, you simply won't win.

If you have other principals in your new venture, give some thought to what you would do if they decided to leave or were called away by illness, death, or change in interests. It's a good idea to consider getting "key-man insurance" to protect the company in case of the sudden demise of a valuable employee.

Another item to consider in the small, closely held business venture is what to do with the stock or ownership interests of a co-owner who passes away. In addition to the personal loss of a business associate and the disruption within the company, you may have to deal with the person's spouse or children. They may want a position on the board of directors or may want to actively intervene in the corporate operation. They may want to receive increased dividends, to offset the loss of income.

I know of a situation in which three men started a company as equal shareholders. The company prospered and grew but never went public. After several years, one of the principals dropped out because of family problems, and eventually developed a nervous disorder. Shortly after, the second principal died. The third member, who was the company president, was working his head off to make the corporation grow and he was doing very well. The only problem was, the two families of the other principals were taking away two-thirds of the profits, contributing nothing to the company growth, and consistently arguing with him over the operation of the company. They were taking up too much of his time. They demanded jobs for unqualified sons and daughters who, once on the job, ignored the company president because they knew he had no real power over them. The final result was the president left and started up his own new venture. He was slapped with a conflict-of-interests lawsuit from the other two stockholders, because the company he left went into decline as he carried away clients to his new venture. No one had planned on anyone ever leaving. One can see some justification on both sides, but the conflict destroyed a nice little company.

Situations like this can be avoided by having a buy/sell agreement in which all principals agree that, upon their death, the stock they own is sold to the corporation for a predetermined price or for a percentage of current sales. The company can buy and pay for life insurance policies on the lives of the principals and name the estate of the principals as beneficiary, in return for that person's share in the enterprise. Or, all parties can arrange for each principal to retain his ownership in the corporation, but with the stock becoming non-voting stock if the principal is no longer active in company operations. In this way, the principal can retain ownership in the corporation for his wife and family if he passes on before the company goes public. The surviving principals do not have to put up with interference from the family or heirs of the departed principal, at a time when they least need such problems.

If the company becomes big enough and goes public, the arrangements described above become academic. At that point, the principals will be able to do whatever they want with the stock, and a buy/sell agreement may not be the most advantageous arrangement. You may want to agree that the stock of any deceased owner will be offered to the surviving principals, at 10 percent below current value or even at the full market value, in order to give them the opportunity to maintain a majority voting interest. There are many other ways to plan for departure of the principals in the new business venture. Once again, get good legal advice well in advance of the departures.

One other point should be discussed here. If you are a principal in a new business venture and you have a law office representing your company, it may be a good idea to have another law firm handle your personal interest. It will represent you or your estate in case you ever want to leave the corporation or you pass away. If you leave your corporate *and* personal interests in the hands of the company law firm, the lawyers will have a problem should the company interests and the interests of your estate conflict. In such cases, it is most likely that the lawyers will lean in favor of the corporation.

Retaining one lawyer to represent both interests is about as silly as a man and woman using the family lawyer to handle a "friendly divorce." A friend of mine tried this and was blown out of the water by his lawyer and former wife at the "friendly" divorce proceedings. He escaped with only the shirt on his back.

You might consider a tontine, which is a financial arrangement that is simple and rather romantic. Suriving members receive the departed members' shares until only one member survives. He receives 100 percent of whatever the venture was. It certainly is clear, clean, and easily understood, but I don't recommend it in today's business world.

As the leader of a company, it's up to you to plan for each and every possible eventuality as far in advance as you can. Time rolls on, and if you lose sight of your long-range goals, you will reach your short-range goals and have nowhere to go from there. In other words, don't get so involved in your tactics that you forget about your strategy.

For those of you who have already started a small business venture, I hope this book has made you aware of specific problems that had escaped your attention. For those of you who have not yet gone out on your own but want to do so: If anything written-herein has dissuaded you from trying, then you probably would not have made it anyway. No one can stop the entrepreneur. He will go ahead no matter what the odds may be.

I hope every reader has received a little bit more insight into what entrepreneurs are like, how they think, how they act, and what motivates them. As Thoreau says, they march to a different drummer because they hear a different beat. Entrepreneurs are no better or worse than anyone else. They are what they are. Most are honest, hardworking, self-motivated people, who do what they do for reasons that makes sense to them. Entrepreneurs try new ventures just to find out if they can succeed.

Index